CW00346862

This edition is a reprint by the Tom Leonard Literary Estate

First published in the UK by The Common Breath,
in association with the Tom Leonard Literary Estate.

Copyright © 2021 the Tom Leonard Literary Estate
ISBN: 979-8-6515297-3-5
Cover by Mark Mechan, Red Axe Design
Typeset by Fabio Laniado

passing through

Tom Leonard

Christmas 2023

To Christopher & Jane,

I'm sure Tom would object to being commodified; and for Christmas FFS! but nonetheless here he is.

Love, Duncan, Tara, Corinne & Breann
x.

The last thing I always wanted to do was to define something. Literally. Sometimes the process of creativity is the process of defining, it turns out. So creativity is process, that is the point.

— **from** *Autumn Leaves*

FOREWORD :
The Tom Leonard Literary Estate

This is a reprint of the first edition, produced and edited by Brian Hamill through his publishing imprint *the common breath*. Brian died soon after the book was published. The original publication would not have been possible without Brian's input and this edition is dedicated to the memory of Brian Hamill.

This book came about from searching my father's archive for any unpublished or uncollected work which might be of interest to his readers. He had arranged his work into an archive which is now with the Scottish National Archive.

The book contains work which did not feature in any of his previous collections such as *Outside the Narrative* 2009 (poetry) or *Definite Articles* 2013 (prose), or was written after those dates. The book fills the gap between 2009-2018 for poetry and 2013-2018 for prose, and works from 1982- 2009 not included in his previous books. It spans from *My Way* written in 1982, through to *Autumn Leaves* from 2018, and includes a lot of the poetry featured on his web journal www.tomleonard.co.uk between 2009-14. There is no draft or incomplete work in this book.

The afterword by James Kelman is a revised version of the brilliant speech he made at my Dad's funeral.

Tom is buried with his parents and brother Eric. The poem "passing through", written in 2010, is inscribed on his gravestone.

Michael Leonard

CONTENTS

Foreword

POETRY
AND
PROSE

Opinion of the Press

Those fearless champions of truth who stand for the assertation of social justice and the daily overthrow of the torpitude of mental habit

at the forefront through the nineteenth century and into the twentieth of the struggle for better living conditions for working people, for Irish home rule, for the success of the General Strike, for votes for women

who have always welcomed not only art from and on the side of the working class but have been first to welcome that formally subversive art which does not comfort the literary expert through proffering the crumbs of internal or structural reference to revered literary icons

which champions of truth naturally feature in order of importance *The Glasgow Herald, The Scotsman, The Guardian, The Independent, The Daily Telegraph, The Times Literary Supplement, The Observer, The London Review of Books, Fanny Craddock's Bumper Book of Doughnuts, The Old Wanker* (formerly *The New Statesman*), *The Times Educational Supplement (Scotland)*

whose combined literary opinions no intelligent post-diluvian would scorn, but mention with rather a serious face and hushed tones in public houses, or consider of significance to leatherbooted dudes impersonating Sean Connery in Great Western Road whose literary editors having discussed this book in conclave now solemnly opine:

—larger than life, it is smaller than the cosmos only by that volume which you now hold in your hand.

THIS BOOK IS ALL THAT IT IS NOT

Poetry Please!

for whom poetry is
a warm cup of cocoa
held to their bosoms

& who go hmmm..... hmmmm.....
at public readings

as if a cow's tongue
was licking their genitals

vanitie

I thought my book was a place for my spirit to be

finally

if that was vanitie

forgive me   I thought it was creativity

that it was meant to be

for all of us

                                    that simple thing

"it is play that is the universal"

                              no   not here

                              not in this place

the primacy of The Word

                              the Patriarch

                              grim reaper

at a poetry reading

he wears his profundity on his sleeve;
he was the man, he suffered—
he was there:

and now, I am here
and you are there
and you are there very much
in your own sense of presence

at being here
and I am beginning to suffer
at your being here too
instead of there.

oh I wish you were back there
I'm sorry it's rotten but
I wish you were back there
and I was still here

alone with the potted plants
and the polite audience
and Life which is a hoot
it's fandabbydozy

and it's been like that
since they first held me upside down
and I started roaring
with laughter

oh bad faith bad faith
cried surgeon magee
but me dear old mammy
whispered sweetly to me

authenticity will out
with or without
a smile on its face

The Elect

one of those with quiet, naturally restrained, insistently mono-
tone voices

with that little selfcontained smile, always going on about respect
for history and the abiding sense of the traditional

who want poets to show a sense of "basic form" and are forever
quoting Yeats's "Under Ben Bulben" about poets having to learn
their trade and not be all out of shape from toe to top

who think this nothing to do with Yeats on eugenics: "the better
stocks have not been replacing their numbers" ..."the results are
already visible in the degeneration of literature"...

who complain of voices yclept loud, various, opinionated, the in-
sufferably "engaged" the political johnnies the performance crowd
the "disastrous influence of the sixties" Ezra Pound no no no Rob-
ert Frost The Road Not Taken (but they all bloody take it) yes yes
yes

who hold fast to Aristotle's dictum that a poet is a poet insofar as
they have a command of metaphor, and who hate poets who carry
electrical appliances onto the stage

who want nothing about "the page as a field of semantic tension"
or "the connection between lower case and democracy" or "the
punctuation of spacing" or "the reader being present at the shared
point of articulation"

one of them leant over and said to me quietly

do you know if the 44 bus still goes to Knightswood

Two Scenes and Two Monologues
from a Work In Progress

Darkness. The opening of Nielsen's overture 'Helios', from its very quiet begin-
ning to its sudden rushing climax that depicts the full splendour of the risen sun:
time 4.5 minutes. Throughout this quiet opening Alice, spot lit, addresses the
audiences, her address finishing just before the orchestral climax occurs.

Alice:
Once upon a time, there were three flying ducks on the wall of a
Glasgow living room. The living-room was papered in diagonal
rows of pretty bunches of flowers, and the ducks were made of
glazed china. The ducks flew permanently north-east above the
bed-settee, between the door to the lobby, and the display-cabinet.
The living-room, the ducks, the bed-settee, the display-cabinet –
these all existed in the head of the small-time Glasgow writer, of
semi-humorous and semi-avantgarde habits.

It happened one day that this small-time writer was attending a
run-of-the-mill sound-poetry festival in Amsterdam. He was saun-
tering down Eerste van der Heltsraat, turning a sound-text over in
his head; being a semi-humorous fellow, he had a notion to present
a spoof chamber piece that evening, which he was to call 'Beetho-
ven's Ninth'; this he had allegedly scored for tenor, dead mouse,
used contraceptive, bunch of grapes and banana.

He was having quiet a chuckle to himself when he was the
source of his mirth by his companion that afternoon, an old
Glasgow acquaintance who had taken up residence in the City of
Tulips. This acquaintance was a tall, middle-aged fading hippie,
who had drunk four bottles of Carlsberg Special and smoked two
joints in honour of his friend's arrival. But when the small-time
writer divulged his reasons for amusement, his irate companion
upbraided him for being a wee petty-bourgeois wanker who had
sold out to the London brigade, and biffed him on the side of the
head. Such was the force of this blow, that inside the writer's head,
the ducks fell from the wall.

8

The music reaches its climax and stops abruptly on that climax, the sound being transformed into the loud roar of aeroplane engines. Lights up shows the three cockpits of three planes flying in close formation, the occupants helmeted and goggled.

Ginger: How far away is this place, Biggles?

Biggles: Oh crumbs, Germany isn't it?

Ginger: Yes. Think so sir.

Biggles: Well for God's sake point the plane in the right direction. We're supposed to be putting on quite a show there tonight. Yes. The old Britannic lion's going to show her teeth. Safety belt fastened?

Ginger: Roger. Biggles.

Biggles: Socks on?

Ginger: Roger.

Biggles: Vest?

Ginger: Vest on sir.

Biggles: Goggles?

Ginger: What?

Biggles: Sorry I mean pants. God. That word.

Ginger: Sir.

Biggles: That damned word, Ginger. *(with difficulty)* Pants. I can't say it. It just sort of brings me out in a cold sweat.

Ginger: It's just an ordinary word, sir. Like goggles. Or vest.

Biggles: I know, Ginger. Don't tell me. Just a sound. The sound caused by a specific vibration of vocal chords in the larynx. But it's its referent, Ginger. In the real world, I mean. Of language, that is. As understood, in the common world of men. And where would we be without that, eh, Ginger. I mean those.

Ginger: Just ignore it, sir. You can call my pants goggles, if you like.

Biggles: Oh no, that wouldn't do. That wouldn't do at all.

	Not playing the game.
Ginger:	Flak to starboard, sir.
Biggles:	45 degrees. Just a touch. Yes. If you take language on board, you take it all. It's the world, you know.
Ginger:	The what?
Biggles:	The world, Ginger.
Ginger:	Roger, sir.
Biggles:	No, just because you don't like the sky one morning, doesn't mean you pretend there's nothing over your head.
Ginger:	45 degrees, sir.
Biggles:	Roger. There are those things one just is saddled with. They have a private referent, however distasteful. I know what it is, too. I just had difficulty with toilet training, when I was a mite.
Ginger:	Alice.
Biggles:	It's the sort of thing a chap doesn't really want to talk about. And an awful lot of chaps repress the memory I'm told. That's where the old subconscious comes in.
Ginger:	Alice.
Alice:	*(in third cockpit)* Roger Ginger.
Biggles:	And language takes over. The imagery always gives a fellow away. The fingerprints of the psyche, Ginger. Written on the wind. Every time a fellow opens his mouth. Or puts pen to paper.
Ginger:	Alice. Are you busy, Alice?
Alice:	I'm reading a newspaper.
Biggles:	I remember standing in a basin in the sink, my auntie washing my bottom.
Ginger:	What's the forecast, Alice?
Alice:	This paper doesn't have a horoscope.
Biggles:	Terrible the way these things affect one's whole life. One can't know it at the time, of course.
Ginger:	Very funny, Alice. The weather you nit.
Biggles:	And here I am piloting a plane to Germany. And I can't say...
Ginger:	Goggles, sir.

Biggles:	Roger, Ginger.
Alice:	Fog over France. Distance 500 kiloms. Clearing through Germany.
Biggles:	Still, it's given me a remarkable understanding of the existential tradition. Lermontov, Barbusse, *La Nausee* – that sort of thing.
Ginger.	Roger, Alice.
Biggles:	"Things have broken free from their names, eh?" By thunder. I didn't have to read a bloody book to haul that chappie from under the bed. Insight, that's what I've got.
Alice:	Ginger.
Biggles:	It's the way the world works, you know. Principle of compensation.
Ginger:	Roger, Alice.
Biggles:	Doesn't matter a damn the source of one's insight into a phenomenon. It's the truth or otherwise of the insight itself.
Ginger:	Roger, Biggles.
Alice:	There's a very interesting article here on dialectical materialism.
Ginger:	Sorry?
Alice:	I said there's a very interesting article here on dialectical materialism.
Ginger:	What the hell's that. What paper are you reading, Alice?
Biggles:	I'll never forget the excitement of first reading Kierkegaard's words about a chap having something he was unable to confess; something that singled him out irrevocably as *that* individual ...
Alice:	It's called *Newsline*, Ginger.
Biggles:	Still – I've confessed now, haven't I? Sort of.
Ginger:	Newsline? Never heard of it. I thought you took the *Bulletin*, or the *Sketch*.
Biggles:	Keep this under your hat, will you, Ginger. It's funny the things one talks about on a run like this. The intimacy. Perhaps the thought one might never come home.

Alice:	It's the newspaper of the Workers' Revolutionary Party.
Ginger:	Jesus Christ. In the name of all that's wonderful, why are you reading *that* muck?
Alice:	I've joined.
Biggles:	I once flew with a surgeon over the Gobi Desert–
Ginger:	Biggles.
Biggles:	– the tank was running short of juice. All of a sudden he opened up about this rubber doll he kept —
Ginger:	Biggles.
Biggles:	Eh?
Ginger:	Biggles. Alice has joined the Workers' Revolutionary Party.
Biggles:	Alice. Come in, Alice.
Alice:	Roger, Biggles.
Ginger:	She's a Trot. The swine's a Trot.
Biggles:	Alice. What's all this nonsense about parties.
Ginger:	The bastard's a Trot. They're everywhere.
Alice:	I've joined the W.R.P., Biggles. I was very impressed with the party's opinions in its newspaper, *Newsline*.
Ginger:	Everywhere. And I'm damned if I'm having a Trot with me bombing Germany.
Alice:	It's a good mix of contemporary scientific and political analysis. And it's got a fine sports section thrown in. Nothing po-faced.
Biggles:	Oh, come on, Alice. Pull yourself together, woman. This is no time for pranks. You know my views on horsing around on a sortie. You'll get us *all* pranged.
Alice:	I'm not horsing around, Biggles. I'm serious.
Ginger:	She'll be telling us all this show's just a crisis of capitalism next.
Biggles:	You damned little shite, Alice.
Alice:	That's a bit thick, sir.
Biggles:	You steaming great turd. You infernal toaly. You –
Ginger:	Biggles.

Biggles:	Alice, all your mouth is brown. You –
Ginger:	Biggles. Imagery, sir.
Biggles:	Eh?
Ginger:	Goggles, sir.
Biggles:	Ah. Roger, Ginger. Crumbs.
Alice:	I think you ought at least to give the party a fair hearing, sir. You ought to read a copy of *Newsline*.
Alice:	Something on radar, sir. Looks like a Hun.
Biggles:	Let's have a look at him. How far do you reckon, Ginger?
Ginger:	About two miles starboard, sir. Approaching fast.
Alice:	You can't judge a party till you've found out what it actually stands for, sir. And you can't trust a word of what the *Bulletin* or the *Sketch* says.
Biggles:	Come on, you swastika-swathed cur! Let's have you, Jerry!

(The sound of another aircraft approaching and roaring past. The sound of Morse Code on the radio)

	Where the devil is he? I want to blast the lily-livered swine from the sky!
Alice:	You see, in today's issue there's a really interesting article.
Ginger:	He's signalling on radio, sir.
Biggles:	What?
Alice:	It's on the relation of dialectical materialism to quantum physics; in particular, to the wave-particle debate.

(During Alice's words, the sound of Morse Code has been followed by the sound as of something whistling the slow movement of Beethoven's Quartet Opus 132)

Ginger:	Oh. Pee. You. Ess. One. Three. Two. Opus 132, sir. Does that mean anything to you?
Biggles:	He's trying to decoy us. The cunning little devil. I'll give him opus 132. Don't worry, Jerry. I'm not

	put off *my* guard!
Alice:	That to understand that matter is constantly in motion is essential to an understanding of the process of historical change.
Biggles:	Rat-tat-tat-tat! Rat-tat-tat-tat! Got you, you bastard!
Ginger:	Good shot, sir!
Alice:	And Lenin's analysis of Hegelian philosophy is consistent with the discoveries of twentieth century physics.
Biggles:	Roger, Ginger. Alice.
Alice:	Which refutes the idealistic basis of twentieth century bourgeois philosophy.
Biggles:	Alice.
Alice:	Roger, Biggles.
Biggles:	Now look here, Alice. I want this Newsline nonsense to stop. We're on A.i. sortie tonight, and it's gen. from H.Q that we put on a good show. I'm not having it filtering back to the top brass that you've joined the Workers' Revolutionary Party.

(Alice's plane moves closer)

Alice:	You ought to have a glance at this article. It should interest you, sir.
Biggles:	I am not. Repeat not. Interested.
Alice:	Are the British always fair, sir?
Biggles:	Of course. Read the history of Ireland.
Alice:	Good. Then you'll understand my position more if you have a read at this yourself, Biggles.

(Alice leans from her cockpit and hands a copy of Newsline to Biggles)

Biggles:	You'll be carpeted for this, Alice.
Ginger:	Creep.
Alice:	It's on page six. Part of a series. It's pretty dense reading, but worth thinking about.
Ginger:	*(Looking across)* Seems to have a nice sports section.

	Colour photographs, eh?
Biggles:	Let's have a look.
Alice:	Oh, you can sneer, but why shouldn't it have? That's a regular feature, full-colour photographs of football players.
Biggles:	Shut up, Alice. We can make up our own minds. Get on with your work.
Alice:	Roger, sir.

(Her plane moves away)

| Biggles: | You know Ginger, I'm blowed if I'm interested in quantum physics, but football strips ... There's another kettle of fish. |
| Ginger: | Sir. |

(As the scene progresses, the noise and flashes from anti-aircraft fire become louder and more regular)

Biggles:	When this wretched war is over, Ginger, I'm going to go home, climb the stairs to my bedroom, and, slowly, and with great satisfaction, pull on a Coventry City football strip.
Ginger:	Roger, sir.
Biggles:	It's got lovely shiny green shorts and a yellow jersey, with yellow stockings.
Ginger:	Roger, Biggles.
Biggles:	And I'll lie and let Rosemary stroke my bum.
Ginger:	Gosh.
Biggles:	Do you like football strips, Ginger?
Ginger:	Oh, I don't know, sir ... I prefer my airman's kit actually!
Biggles:	Very proper, Ginger. Very patriotic. Still, I've always loved a good football strip. Next to Coventry I think I'd have Brazil. It's those light blue...
Ginger:	Goggles, sir.
Biggles:	Roger, Ginger. And long clingy white stockings are always rather fun. The way they grasp one's

calves, you know? It's something to do with the fibres ... And I think I prefer the little diamond piped down the side rather than the three close lines ... Which sports firm is that? I can never re-member. Alice.

Alice: Roger, sir.

Biggles: What's the name of the firm that pipes the little diamonds down the sides of football strips?

(The sound of a terrific explosion. Darkness. Various cries of consternation.)

Ginger: Sir, we've been hit!

Biggles: Parachutes everyone! We're pranged!

(Scene 2: Biggles and Ginger enter, Ginger as a priest. Too embarrassed to confess in English, Biggles confesses in Latin)

Biggles: Ehm... et putavi de emh... de togibus ludeendo-rum ehm... et ejaculavi ehm...

Ginger: For Christ's sake shut up. People like you should have their prick done in a toastie.

Biggles: But I need absolution, father.

Ginger: Absolution my arse. I know you, son. I know your type. You don't realise the Church has changed a lot since the days you were in it. Creeping around stuffed to the eyebrows with sexual guilt, thinking you're some kind of unique speck of grit in the cosmic machine. All because you tug your wire over some mental outfit that isn't a straight feel-the- breasts-hump-the-fanny deal. Fuck me, son, stop giving yourself a hard time.

Biggles: But my conscience won't leave me alone, father.

Ginger: Balls. That's all balls. Psychosis at a peep. Turn the gas off, you'll find the air easier to breathe. And stop calling me father. I'm not your father, and this patriarchy thing of yours is one obses-sion that's really beginning to get on my tits. Very Scottish, isn't it? Daddy this, daddy that.

	MAAAAaaammy!
Biggles:	I know what I'll be – I'll be a writer!

(In the following dialogue Biggles, Ginger and then Alice are stage lit as standing in a three-flying-ducks position)

Ginger:	Christ all these fucking late calls and letters to the papers about headmasters and what will they think of us abroad and school uniform and –
Biggles:	That's it. I'll write a novel. I'll write a novel about this angry young man who's been so, God, he's so repressed in his childhood, but my God he is sensitive. My God, he's so sensitive he goes for these long walks on his bleak council estate and –
Ginger:	– and letters to the *Scotsman* about The Correct Form of Highland Dress and people spending half their lives passing ten thousand volts through dead language and all this shite about Scottish sojers and fucking war memorials on half the school walls of their big dour prison-like schools and –
Biggles:	– and he learns off by heart *Portrait of the Artist as a Young Man* and then he has this terrible argument with his best friend about Transubstantiation then he goes to Mass and sits right under the priest letting everybody see he's reading Freud's *The Future of an Illusion* and –
Ginger:	– and all this Catholic Protestant Catholic Catholic Protestant shite with nobody saying crack about a big fucking capitalist football club bang smack in the middle not signing one single Catholic oh no nudge wink wink I mean Duke of Edinburgh's a fucking grand master isn't he lads and –
Biggles:	– this priest is a real big baw-faced think that starts going on about Communism and people getting involved in politics and how he once knew a woman that got this Labour Party pamphlet through her door and she got quite interested seeing that she knew anyway it's not as if they're the Unionist

	party and wasn't it them that got approval for the
	separate Catholic schools so it's almost you duty
	and -
Alice:	Course you can't really help wondering if he's just
	on some big sexist ego trip to show you really ab-
	ject. Mind you get used to it as long as he's washed
	it for Christ's sake –
Biggles:	– she went along to this Labour Party branch
	meeting one night and they seemed a nice bunch
	of folk they were just like anybody you would
	meet in the street and there was this young chap
	with a beard who started talking to her and they
	went for a cup of coffee and just before she went
	to have a bite of her kit-kat she went to say a wee
	grace-before- meals as usual and this young chap
	had said –
Ginger:	– mind he was probably in the Boys Brigade the
	wee mason as they're known in the trade get it
	young get it hot (*imitates a trumpet*) root-toot-toot-
	toot-toot-toot; root-toot-toot-toot-toot-toot stead-
	fast by fuck oh aye which hope we have as an
	anchor of the soul both sure and steadfast and
	which entereth that within the veil Hebrews six
	nineteen –
Alice:	– the first time it was like peeling back an old elas-
	toplast and there was this sort of soapy stuff under
	the mushroom lid and he started rolling it up be-
	tween his forefinger and thumb and sniffing it he
	says he sometimes does that when he's reading a
	book it helps him relax and –
Biggles:	– you don't still believe in all that nonsense do you
	he'd said and he'd started on about how religion
	had always been the true enemy of the working
	classes and the priests and the bishops and even
	the pope that's correct even our holy father the
	pope
Ginger:	– land the good jobs that's their fucking hope oh
	aye times of high unemployment right enough

no highers have you eh that's not so good still I see you're sure and steadfast laddie start on monday root-toot-toot-toot-toot-toot-toot oh aye the wee masons that's what my mother called them still that duke of edinburgh never had to start on monday that big bastard no wonder they called him the duke of fucking edinburgh where else marco polo that's the cunts real name marco polo and the rest –

Alice: – it's just it's funny on the edges of your teeth the way the skin's still quite mobile but underneath there's like this sort of bone cylinder I mean it's like the way your finger shoogles back and forward if you press on the skin over the breastbone of an uncooked chicken –

Biggles: the natural successor to peter to whom christ had said upon this rock I will build my church our holy father the pope on whom the holy spirit had conferred the gift of infallibility in all matters of faith and morals and anyway this guy the sensitive one not the one with the beard stands up and shouts at this big baw-faced thick with the dog-collar that is a load of shite that is a load of fucking keech –

Ginger: - and granny with the head-tilted smile and the great admiration for Ian Smith bastard millions stashed away in south Africa no doubt no wonder she's smiling and her daughter and charles and that fucking mirang he married how many millions elizabeth plus charles plus diana leave it at that how many millions write it out in numbers how many millions where is it all silently working away why are all these bastards roped together on the one mountain all turning with their heads tilted at the angle smiling –

Alice: – but you have to watch when he's going his dinger that he doesn't shove it down your throat and make you sick –

(In a monologue from further on in the play, another character, For Fuck's Sake, recalls the poetry scene in Glasgow in the sixties.)

For Fuck's Sake:
I mind well those heady days, when the world seemed an oven-fresh hot cross bun, and Parsifal was an opera by Wagner. There was a bunch of men then, by God we were men, and we were the rising thing. Every day you could bump into a poet on the streets of the city, and by thunder you had to say sorry, or he would stretch you out cold. You know, Glasgow was a virgin then – a raddled old virgin whore stretched out waiting for twenty talented pens to write her up. And write her up we did.
It was the place, and the *placeness* of the place. You know, making a poem in those days, a man reached for his saw and held the grain of the wood to his eye, to see that it was true. Every dunny was the Frontier of Art, and smokeless zones let the city's poets gaze up at the stars. We wandered the city streets by day, feeling the city-streetness of the city streets, the *dayness* of the day. And sometimes half-crazed with the very thingness of the whole thing, we'd gather in some mean old backyard at dusk, and cook trout and beans under a Glasgow moon. We'd lie there, stretched out and deep in measured talk, till the Plough had faded from the skies over Charing Cross, and our wives were fast asleep facing the wall. We'd talk about the craft, we'd talk about the materials, we'd talk about our *tools... (thoughtfully fingers the banana.)*

Being Scottish

They don't want you being Scottish.
They want you "having Scots".

This means having

educated yourself
out of a workingclass way of talking;

that's all "slang","ugly", macho even:
no – hold on a bit. "Glasgow Scots"

is the newly accepted mudhut
in the Scots Language landscape

now in these nationalist days that
hate to call themselves nationalist.

The Cesspit and the Sweetie Shop, Westminster and Hollyrood 2014

The Cesspit

The government was run
by one who had made his
career in Public Relations,
and Public Relations was the
ever-there, the oil and glue
of what had been, and
Public Relations maintained
was still, representative
parliamentary democracy.
But representative of what,
and whom, and which?

Of Public Relations itself
it seemed, a not-quite empty
set of had-to-be recorded
signs and actions, running
parallel but contrary to what
people knew and experienced.
A ritual: the acquired signs
of meaning and personal
sincerity outwardly shown
by rote: a ritualisation of the
concept of democracy and
dialogue, masquerading as
dialogue and democracy itself.

People outside the lateral
inter-relationship of Press
and politics felt somehow
the world they knew had
nothing to do with the world
they saw and heard reported.
Endless the flip-chart mentality
about nought point five or was it
eight of "growth"; "experts"
from thinktanks were the norm,
never the ordinary daily rising
cost of food seen in the shops,
the gas, the electric bills long
since gone crazily upward.
Historic societal conflict
was redefined, no longer
rich versus poor, worker
against employer, capital
versus labour. The culture
and its language had been
systematically changed.
Granted, historic injustices
of men over women, white
over black, straight over
gay were taken up and
countermanded in part
by law; but never in such
a way as to question the
new ubiquitous orthodoxy,
the daily myth proposed
of central societal struggle:

"the taxpayer" versus the
drain on the taxpayer's tax.

Everything was done for public relations
the language-sets, their perameters;
how the hands were clasped at the front
in interview, calling the interviewer by
their first name. And well they might,
they probably knew each other intimately,
dined in the same clubs, flourished in the same
earnings band, each knew their job to be
management of the language environment,
an integral part of managing the economy:
managing the economy that would
preserve their place within it as it stood.

Their wars were the same:
structural templates of PR
grounding a rolling
multi-countried occupation,
bombardments manned or
unmanned with internal
surveillance always allegedly
keeping the people safe;
just like the wars, just like
the occupations, just like
the bombardments manned
or unmanned said to be
"keeping the people safe."

The Sweetie Shop

A clear majority won
its first re-branding was
the name "government"
itself; decreed and taken up
forthwith by public media
as if the undisputed
and indisputably apposite
title for what had been
till then not government
at all but simply "executive"
with ten percent of power.
For self-styled government,
the question now
became, as time went by
—How come our government
has only ten percent?
Not nationalisation was
the answer, but a corporate
nationalism, whose logos
over an upbeat language
of business-diploma jargon
sprinkled with mission-statement
bullet-points, pervaded the
public bumf and websites
of this now-government's
areas of funded operation.
A sleekit mantra of jaunty
national pride became
de trop in public titles,
unnoticed largely, and

uncommented on, by
those who spread the word.
The word was "Scotland".

Titles across the range
of public life were binned
in root-and-branch reshaping
to present a consciousness
of stand-alone nationhood,
the nation's name declared
over and again in endstop
affirmation: *Sport Scotland*,
Education Scotland; while
"Strathclyde Police" like other
regional departments, its
headed paper, its public signs,
all that which gave it separate
identity, now was removed,
subsumed under the one
Police Scotland—albeit, creepily,
"police" be a transitive verb. What
do you do for a living, Sir Constable?
"I police Scotland," he said.

Artists became "creatives",
a bright and cheery term,
Creative Scotland sounded
nothing of grump or ivory tower;
amang its website bullet-points

and paths to artistic outcomes,
came news that one in four awards
would now be for work in *Scots*:
in case some glaikit southron chiel
had nay notion, links in English
were given to sites explaining
this "national language" that
folk were supposed to scrieve in.

Across the travelling country
carriages brandished the
upbeat logo "Scotland's Railways";
even Jock Tamson's abused
had public institutional help renamed
Survivor Scotland. The pensioner's
bus pass no longer named a region
but bore *One Scotland* over
the national flag. Each time the pass
was daily used, the message, time
and again and again: *One Scotland,*
over the national flag.

The taboo word for card-carrying
nationalists was nationalism
itself. That word would put off
too many folk it was better to
keep onside. That which the
nationalists had been striving for
for eighty years had finally been

forced to a national crunch: and,
in a hyper-canny sleight-of-hand
worthy indeed of parliamentary
politics, it was all, in the end,
supposedly nothing to do with *them*.

For some on the Left
the Parliamentary Road
to Socialism was up
and running again.
Not since the days of
Militant in pre-New
Labour had they had
such a spring in their
step. It was a time for
leafletting and demos,
fervour at sorting out
Labour's traitors once
and for all, Get rid of
those traitorous vipers
and their one-party rule
in the West. Smash the
British State was the cry,
throw off the yoke of
Imperialism. Throw off
the yoke? Lay aside
the reins more like, the
Empire had already
thrown off its yoke, but
not with any help from

Scotland and its *bonny*
fechters the warld ower.
On the other hand
the "no" camp
was a gallimaufray
of horrors, the
gibbering dead up
from Westminster
wrapped in the
union flag; beside
them skinheads
from the BNP,
with every hue
of far-right politic
to deepest Orange.

Rightly these said
that 1707 and the
Protestant Crown
over a single
union parliament
was chosen guarantee
of independence
from Rome over
independence from
England. Union
was itself that
guarantee. Did not
Burns himself in 1793
write that the monarch

"to speak Masonic,
is the keystone in
our royal arch
constitution"?

But Burns was
tholing his boss
for thinking him
radical; fighting
to keep his job
to feed his weans.
He was a Mason
when so was
Catholic Haydn
and Mozart of
the Requiem Mass
besides his great
masonic opera
The Magic Flute.

for Eddie as always, on his 90ᵗʰ

yi dancin   ur

izzit jist thi wey yir stonnin

                yi stonnin
                ur
                is it jist the wey yir dancin

the wey yir dancin

                the wey yir stonnin

                        dancin   eddie
                        eddie   dancin

stonnin eddie
eddie stonnin

                happy birthday eddie dancin

                happy birthday eddie stonnin

                  stonnin dancin
                  eddie morgan

a reply to a masculinist

being itself is more important than the name for it
being itself is more important than the word for it

being is quick
being is of the quick
being is not that-which-is-owned

judge not lest/
stuck in the word
text

text without space
that which is grasped

a grasping
a person who grasps

owning

the man here owns the world
to himself

to his idea of self
this male owns the world to himself
in his idea of self

self is word
self is identity
imposition of order

no more the subconscious structured as a language

this man is weighed down

he has to carry the world in his word
he has to explain the word to the world

this man thinks he is a man
to himself

therefore
he has to carry the world in his word

but being itself is more important than the name for it
being itself is more important than the word for it

text

space

My Way

Though some maintain
the Real Presence
from here
to Rawalpindi

I decided at
an early age
that Transubstantiation
wuz oot the windy

though it might seem
a pastor's dream
and bishops thought
my logic shoddy

I burned my boat
I turned my coat
became a Proddy

        though some may mock
        the macho talk
        upon the Walk
        of No Surrender

        I've drunk the rent
        I've clocked the wife
        I've spewed my ring
        upon the fender

I've had the shakes
I've had D.T's
I've fell asleep
upon the chanty

I've woke to see
upon my knee
the Works of Dante

I've seized that cup
called Life's Spatoon
I've spooned it up
yes, gulped it doon

I am a man
not one of them
who flee in fear
Life's Bowls of Phlegm

though in the dumps
I've chewed the lumps
I've chewed them my way

I've turned again
back to my faith
my banner Truth
at last unfurled

my mission plain
before I die
to spread these words
throughout the world

toffolux queen
chopin's cuisine
that rare frissoang
ring-a-ding-doang

sumdy's farted
proportional representation
fa-a-at bo-oab

the pluperfect case
a sweaty groin
a pound of links
the russian ballet

chelsea seven
east stirling one
e=mc squared
a close so wally

god bless our pope
legalise dope
I'd like a grope
u-upyir jacksy

The Aquarian – for Eddie Linden

The base the same:
the place
set out from, returned
to always there.

Not the place of origin
worn on the sleeve and/or
in the larynx;
nor the childhood saddled with.

Nor metropolitan litterati
tholed,
benignly patronising
"incorrigible provincial character"
"rough diamond" shit;
bolstering
imagined counterpoint.

That can pass
a handy hour
in decoy.

It gets boring but.

In reality it's consistency
of application;
focus of belief,

concern outside the self
held, over a lifetime.

yirraw right, Eddie
–yill day

you're all right, Eddie
you'll do

here's tay yi
here's to you

Londoner

on 3 score & 10

restore the place

restore
      the place meta-place
      assert

                    native as native
                    inner is native

      assert
           despite   (in despite of)

the colonial voice   : implacable
                        institutionally hermetic

                  gathered-into-itself
                    as displacing native
                          "naturally"

                    the institutional
                    gathered-into-itself
                    supplanting

        the force of the idiolect
                    locally connected

hear, see, feel, touch :   assert
                          the native
                          nascor / to be born

CUT WELFARE!

SAVE THE WARFARE STATE!

The Scottish Nationalist Guide to Socialism

sequence: from a remote place

(1)

where we go
            sepa
                    rately across

                    the day
                    swings over

                                the usual

                                though
                    always

                            separate
                    always

                    (the day)

(2)

we cling   /   they cling

to the behaviour

patterns of identity   :   how else

not to think , sift

      the second by second by second

   the light on the wall

   ~~the~~ wave

      ~~crashing~~

      on the shore

(3)

the given

shaken   the change

                     of atmosphere

                     into – the – present

the defining place

all present

                     where it occurs

                     again

                     that defines the again

                     never

never   ever   never

                     the defining

(4)

there we went
     Derwent

              the faces
              looking up the well

              looking up the well

        down
        down

              it will come
              it will come

only the present

        not moving

        only the present

                the external
            folk moving

(5)

to save myself

~~to save myself~~

~~from being~~

~~myself as only object~~

~~what is~~

~~the sense of~~ :

space at last ,

~~space to breathe:~~   ~~to construct~~

one's own narrative

---

writing
to save myself
through process
of becoming
witnessed
to myself
an
actuality

(6)

             the untrue vision

not

~~the reverse helix~~

        goodness

        ~~generated to~~

            infinity

                from

          ~~building~~

          ~~generating~~

        ~~the other side~~

        ~~justice revealed~~

~~its opposite~~

~~particles of~~

~~reflection~~

~~this what you observe~~

~~not-I~~

~~gone over~~

(7)

<u>n</u> has become

                  $n - 1$; tending

                        ~~tove~~ towards N

this is how to see it

       perhaps

                   to objectify

towards behaviour-pattern concept

this is ^{would be} _{seeing pre-determined}

~~falin~~ falling-into-patterning

          denial of

their own regard for their

              haeccitas

(8)

only
in this place ~~to defend~~

the construction

of what is
that becomes
evident before the eyes
not given;

that reassures
in that forgetting
in that   being-who-I-am
in the ~~woel~~ world
here

as felt only sense, sense

and being here

a soft

night

               a soft night

    the sea lapping against

                  the moon

(9)

to take control

accept
               forgive
the other:
                         only
                         the words
                                 taking shape
                         in what is

the other remains
        other-but-loved   this

                         the taking shape

                                 is

                         the becoming

                         condemned
                         to be taking shape

forever

is not   —is

(10)

sanity prevails

    ails

        clinging

        to the narrative

        discovering

            the self

            there,

            still

        still

(11)

where we go

        sepa

           rately   across

           the day
           swings over

                       the usual

                       though

           always

                     ~~separate~~

           always

                         (the day)

the myth

(12)

the day

remains

the day

taking shape

for   ever   is

(13)

        the day

        remains

        the day

        taking shape

for   ever   is

        [night]

(14)

the day

remains

the day

taking shape

for   ever   is

(end of sequence)

News from Nowhere

Poison from the radio. The television, a series of electrons hitting the screen, creating an image. Difficult to breathe. Do other people feel like this?

What an insult to language, to have to go around, letting this thing take the place of being in language. Why is there no person in language, do others feel like this too.

Authority, and this not a recollection but the fact of being here, looking at the place, such decent things to see, when the eyes are used, carefully. The colour of Irises.

Just another day, another grey day with nobody of any importance doing anything. Far from the centres of power a member of the masses sits watching television. There is a talk-in about anxiety this is rather a serious subject for this series. Gripping. If you agree phone a thousand digits if you're in Glasgow or Belfast change the first three accordingly.

Retrospective Preface
to the Phonetic Poems

nor tribe not nation
but community
  —& the music
of its language-pool

Two Old Hospital Poems

On the Side

yes the luxury
of being alone not
waking anybody
sitting up to write

at odd hours only
here in bed 3 am
getting the idea over and

across knowing if the
temperature changes in the
mind too much just

get out of bed pad
down the corridor and
ask for another diazepam

The Room

this is who I am, this place
commonly owned
and not
by the passers through :

at last
nothing with my spoor on it,
everything public, my name
a card on the door .

make the most of it
while time slips by
& far in the dark
the lights are on at home

dona nobis pacem

GONNY
GIE US
PEACE

THE GREAT REFERENDUM DEBATE

CHAPTER FOUR HUNDRED AND EIGHTY TWO

The Daily Fruits of Empire

wake

seretide 250.

bran flakes, toast with marmalade. A banana.
tiotropium 18. aspirin 75.

venlafaxine 75.
medium latté with blueberry muffin.
lansoprosole 30.

terbutaline sulphate 500 (if desired).

bisoprolol fumarate 5.
baked potato, salmon, broccoli.
tea. one orange, 2 tea biscuits.

atorvastatin 20
tea. toast with jam.
amisulpride 50 (if desired)

seretide 250

sleep

Memory of Fuerteventura

we walked into the sun
along the shore

my lungs
were fine

        and so
        was the day

        to be in

[home thoughts from abroad]

bored by it all. Switched off,   :

only music, & what there is of poetry

        the love of my children
        who live too far away

        in their own lives

        :

nothing to posit, to say positive:

        "they're all the same"
        --presumption)

so am I
who have no cause to stand over

        the eejits grazing "celebrities"
        "   "   "today's events"
        "   "   "moral outrage"

        so am I
        who have nothing to say

half four in the morning

        well past the middle of life
        & come to a clearing in the forest

ma innermost grunn
is a musical base

     its groundin in silence
          its measure in space

the word for the image
an infinite trace

          its sound of its silence
          ma innermost place

the

mark

of

isolation

is

the

sheltering

grace

of

all

yet here "I" am, still

banished from the word
                          leave it
alone for your   self (that old thing)

citing a then-present
state of mind
        as found object
        aggregate collocation;

the habitué pathologist
classifies
rather than face, ever accept
        continuity over consequence:

                easier to classify
                dissociation

as symptom,
 --index of source
its closure, its summation:

        yet here "I" am

        still in the present
        of "your" understanding

 if capable
 of it: are you?

the hour
stands
at the foot of the bed

B.V.
-time to move on

fragment *Bank Street, Tom McGrath's place 1969*

it seemed a time
> when things were going forward
>> we were young and together

much to discuss
> that came from America
>> not from Scotland

full of old men
> bitter wee fights
>> "Scots versus English"

sunbeams from cucumbers
> divorced from their tongue
>> "divorce is the sign of our times"

the politics of place
> the politics of voice
>> the politics of class

a democracy it seemed
> no shit about religion
>> the irish screwing up "our language"

building linguistic moats
> round the Reformation
>> of supposed core "Scottishness"

The Eff word

I have always felt a great antipathy
to the Eff word.

Frotteurism.

It really rubs me up the wrong way.

thinks

maybe it's
just a habit who knows
does it   nearly every day

nthat
becomes the hat
he hangs himself on

so many of them, some paid
some just who knows
etching out of childhood, whatever

whatever

----

the this thing   whatsit
being in the now

well

I mean to say   I mean
saying it

is this just a stop
enroute

habit

----

habituated, is that a word?
habituated to it, not

conscious.
                    conscious?

maybe word is just a habit
etching out of childhood, oh right

whatever.

----

many are called

many are called
but few are chosen

**maist a yi
urrny getn in**

REVIEWS

Ezra Pound: The Solitary Volcano
John Tytell. Bloomsbury. 1988

Letters of Ezra Pound and Louis Zukofsky
Ed. Barry Ahearn. Faber. 1987

> *Pound talks like no one else. His is almost a wholly original accent, the base of American mingled with a dozen assorted "English society" and Cockney accents inserted in mockery, French, Spanish and Greek exclamations, strange cries and catcalls, the whole very oddly inflected, with dramatic pauses and diminuendos. It takes time to get used to it, especially as the lively and audacious mind of Pound packs his speech – as well as his writing – with undertones and allusions.*

This was Pound described in London where he lived for twelve years after arriving aged 22 from America in 1908; the London years, he told Charles Olson forty years later, were "the high period" of his life.

Tytell shapes his biography into six sections corresponding to the six places Pound stayed in during his life: America ("An American Youth") 1885-1908; London ("Art for Art's Sake") 1908-1920; Paris ("The Heresy of Art") 1920-1924; Rapallo ("The Politics of Art") 1924-1945; Washington, St Elizabeth's Hospital ("The Bedlam of Art") 1945-1958; Rapallo ("The Silent Years") 1958-1972. Taking the average number of biography pages Tytell gives per year of Pound's life in each of these six location-sections, Tytell measures Pound's life as America 1; London 11; Paris 8; Rapallo just over 4; St Elizabeth's about three-and-a-half; and Rapallo again – three-quarters. This not only agrees with Pound's own reckoning as told Olson, but corresponds to Tytell's shaping of Pound's life as that of a tragic hero with apex of influence, and fall.

He describes Pound, in the introduction that prefigures the course of the book and his conclusions, as "..an overly sensitive man who in the midst of a maelstrom had shouted terrible words, absurdly defending some ideal of free speech from a stage while the theatre was burning." Pound's wartime Italian Fascist broadcasts were "an example of what might be called a negative susceptibility, a self-destructive capacity shared by a number of artists."

One can disagree with Tytell's interpretation here, but he gives you plenty of facts clearly enough for you to do so without feeling pressured to take the author's view. Certain specifics are noted in the development of Pound's poetic style: the important episode in 1911 when Pound brought Ford Madox Ford an advance copy of his Canzoni and Ford liter- ally rolled on the floor laughing at the style with its attempt to learn, as Pound later recalled, "the stilted language that then passed for 'Good English' in the arthritic milieu that held control of the respected British critical circles." A year later as European editor of Poetry he was writing to its main editor Harriet Monro in Chicago:

> *Objectivity and again objectivity, and no expression, no hind-side-be-foreness, no Tennysonianness of speech – nothing, nothing, that you couldn't in some circumstance, in the stress of some emotion, actually say. Every literaryism, every book word, fritters away a scrap of the reader's patience, a scrap of his sense of your sincerity.*

By 1913 there was Pound's "A Few Don'ts by an Imagiste" in the March issue of Poetry. Tytell writes of Imagism: "Pound real- ised from the start that Imagism was a finite means to improve the line as a unit in poetry, to curtail the element of discourse in the poem as James had revised the old-fashioned omniscient narrative control in the novel."

The collection Cathay in 1915 Tytell sees as representing an- other technical advance towards the Cantos: "Cathay was an im- portant step for Pound because it allowed him to integrate Imagist technique into a narrative structure." Of course the quoted para- graph at the opening of this review has relevance to the form of the Cantos – as have Pound's letters. The description of the London and Paris years are packed, though not clogged, with the artists and writers whom Pound knew; the book threads the different meeting places, magazines, rivalries. Pound's wide- spread influence on other writers is traced. It was Pound of course who persuaded Harriet Monroe to publish Eliot's Prufrock, and who edited The Waste Land down to the size in which it was published and became known; Eliot, on receiving the $2000 Dial award for the poem, "felt Pound should have received the prize as a recognition of his share in the making of the poem." The acknowledgments from other poets are quoted from their own words, like Joyce's recollection of Pound's help:

> *Ten years of my life have been consumed in correspondence and litigation about my book Dubliners. It was rejected by 40 publishers; three times set up, and once burnt. It cost me about 3,000 francs in postage, fees, train and boat fare, for I was in correspondence with 110 newspapers, 7 solicitors, 3 societies, 40 publishers and several men of letters about it. All refused to aid me, except Mr. Ezra Pound. In the end it was published, in 1914, word for word as I wrote it in 1905.*

Marianne Moore and Wyndham Lewis also came into print via Pound. Friendship with Yeats, begun in London and continued in Paris and Rapallo, where Yeats visited Pound at home, saw the balance of influence tilt from the older to the younger man – though not enough, as far as Pound was concerned. But Yeats's early appreciation of Pound's criticism in their twenty-year relationship is quoted in a letter to Lady Gregory:

> *He is full of the middle ages and helps me to get back to the definite and concrete away from modern abstractions. To talk over a poem with him is like getting you to put a sentence into dialect.*
> *All becomes clear and natural.*

In Paris Hemingway befriended Pound, and later wrote that the poet taught him more about how to write than anyone else in his life. It was Pound "who had taught me to distrust adjectives as I would later learn to distrust certain people in certain situations." Sculptors taken up by Pound included Brancusi and Gaudier-Breszka, whose bust of Pound the poet took to Rapallo, and whose death in the Great War, Tytell implies, contributed to that change of direction when, as Pound recalled, "In 1918 I began an investigation of causes of war, to oppose same." This Tytell calls "the beginning of his disastrous turn from art to the sociology of power and propaganda."

The fourth section of the biography is, like the others, divided into smaller subsections separately titled. The opening subsection title, The Exile, both describes Pound's separation from America and the London-Paris cultural scenes, and refers to the magazine The Exile that Pound launched from Rapallo in 1927. The section describes Rapallo, the location of Pound's house, how he organised his day; Pound's declining reputation, his work on the Cantos; the visits of Yeats and others, the arrival of Basil Bunting to set up house nearby; the letters, three a day or more as the years passed, literally thousands being written from Rapallo during the Thirties: the increasing obsession with C.H. Douglas's theory of social credit, the increasing anti-semitism, the increasing commitment to fascism.

Different aspects of the development of this are previously recorded: Pound's father and grandfather's involvement in the physical making of money; anti-semitism in Pound's childhood home town, Wyncote; the anti-semitism of writers like Eliot, Lewis, Charles Maurras, or of important patrons like the lawyer John Quinn; the racial theories of Leo Frobenius; Pound's friend- ship in 1923 with Lincoln Steffens, who transmitted to Pound his own enthusiasm for Mussolini. The extent of Pound's racialism and commitment to Fascism is made quite clear. His meeting with Mussolini (eulogised in the Cantos) his correspondence both with Mussolini and with economic advisers to Hitler; his work for fascist newspapers in Italy, England, Japan – one article having the title

"The Jews, Disease Incarnate"; his use of the fascist calendar in his letters, signing one such letter (to James Laughlin) "Heil Hitler"; his polemical talks on Rome Radio during the war; his refusal to change his views when taken back to America, though disguising these from those who would have had him executed for treason; his relationships from hospital with people in the "Aryan League of America", and with the American neo-Nazi John Kasper, who affectionately addressed Pound in his letters as "Dear Boss."; his giving the Fascist salute – as a full-page photograph shows – as the ship taking him back to Italy in 1958 approached harbour; his appearance at the head of a neo-Nazi demonstration in Milan as late as 1962, the year of his 77th birthday.

William Carlos Williams – who first met Pound at college in 1903 – was enough influenced by Pound's advocacy of C.H. Douglas's "Social Credit" scheme to speak approvingly of it in 1936 (see "Revolutions Revalued" in A Recognisable Image: William Carlos Williams on Art and Artists New Directions 1978); but fascist racialism was not for W.C.W. Tytell, stating that Williams's thirty-five years in medicine had made him a sharp judge of character, quotes a letter written by Williams to James Laughlin in 1939:

> *The man is sunk, in my opinion, unless he can shake the fog of fascism out of his brain during the next few years, which I seriously doubt that he can do. The logicality of fascist rationalization is soon going to kill him. You can't argue away wanton slaughter of innocent women and children by the neoscholasticism of a controlled economy program. To hell with a Hitler who lauds the work of his airmen in Spain and so to hell with Pound too if he can't stand up and face his questioners on that point.*

The shift in Pound's focus from his arrival at Rapallo is at the centre of the new anthology in Faber's series of Pound's letters, those between himself and Louis Zukofsky. The young Marxist Jewish American (aged 23, Pound 19 years older) sent his "Poem Beginning 'The'" to Pound in Rapallo in 1927. "First cheering mss. I have recvd. In weeks, or months, or something or other," Pound wrote back. The poem duly appeared in the third issue of The Exile, an issue which also included Yeats's "Sailing to Byzantium".

Pound decided, all the way from Italy, that it was time to organise a new young set of writers in New York:

> *I suggest that you form some sort of gang to INSIST on interesting stuff (books) <1.> being pubd promptly, and distributed properly. 2. simultaneous attacks in as many papers as poss. On abuses definitely damaging la vie intellectuelle.*

Pound even offered to help pay for the meals of those who couldn't afford to meet in a cheap restaurant, which is where he suggested the new group should best meet up:

> *restaurant is best, better than studio where complication of host- guest relation arises. Nacherly O.K. to go down to Bill's once or twice if he'll have you.*
>
> *As also the gordarm marital ammosphere of N.Y. Poesy Society !!!!!!!!!!!!!!!!! I be a society. I have officers and by laws. (not that I think this exhortation necessary ...)*
>
> *You've got to have a busy man; lacking one busy by nature, some more contemplative spirit has to take on some of the functions.*

"Bill" was Williams. Though Pound was a bit out of touch with what was going on in literary New York, his having Zukofsky and Williams meet up had important results: Zukofsky began helping Williams edit his poems, notably those that appeared in the collection "The Wedge" of 1944 (the collection whose introduction speaks of a poem as "a machine made of words").

Five years after Pound had been trying to organise a literary movement round Zukofsky in New York, he had become finally disinterested in such schemes. When Zukofsky wrote in 1933 proposing the formation of a group Writers Extant (that became in fact the Objectivist Press) Pound dismissed this curtly: "Le personnel manque// fer yr/ proposed organisation. You ought to read C.H. Douglas."

But before becoming thus disinterested he had, in 1931, obtained for Zukofsky the guest editorship of the Spring 1931 issue of Harriet Monroe's Poetry: Pound's excited response on hearing the news, and the torrent of advice he poured on Zukofsky- a bit too much by the occasional crackle in Zukofsky's response – forms a letter sequence that is a highlight of the book (pp.45-59). As with all the best of Pound's letters, something of that flamboyant verbal character described in 1916 leaps off the page. Most of his correspondents felt driven feebly to emulate it in reply at some point; again, some Black Mountain writers, in their use of capital letters for instance, have turned what was energy into a cliché. But the original remains original.

> *Dear Zuk:*
>
> *Wonners will nevuHH cease. I have just recd. Nooz from Harriet [Monroe] that she is utting you at the wheel for the Spring cruise.*
>
> *I dunno whether in L'annonce fait a L.Z. she mentioned the forefly-ing occasions????*
>
> *At any rate since it was a letter from donal mckenzie that smoked me up into writing Harriet the letter that awoke in her noble booZUMM the fire of enthusiasm that led her to let you aboard*
>
> *I*
>
> *wd. Appreciate it if you wd. Invite mckenzie to do one of the prose articles for the number and state his convictions as forcibly as possibl....*
>
> *after which I see no reason why you shdnt. Add an editorial note saying why you disagree.*
>
> *Poetry has never had enUFF disagreement INSIDE into own wall.*

In the middle of a lively series of collocated points that 80 includes what Pound sees as the difference between Zukofsky's position in 1931 and that of the Imagist group of 1913, he writes:

> *I do not think contributions from ANYone over 40 shd. Be included; and preferably it shd. Be confined to those under 30.*

Three letters poured forth from Rapallo in two days. Zukofsky, after a comparatively flat reply to the sustained barrage of advice, responded item by numbered item to 39 of the points Pound raised. Regarding the prospective age of the contributors, and referring ("H & H") to Pound's recent appearance in the magazine Hound and Horn, he replied:

> *28. Think I'll have as good a "movement" as that of the premiers imagistes – point is Wm. C. W. of today is not what he was in 1913, neither are you if you're willing to contribute – if I'm going to show what's going on today, you'll have to. The older generation is not the older generation if it's alive & up – Can't see why you shd. Appear in the H & H alive with 3 Cantos & not show that you are the (younger) generation in "Poetry." What's age to do with verbal manifestation, what's history to do with it, – good gord lets disassociate ijees – I want to show the poetry that's being written today – whether the poets are of masturbating age or the father of families don't matter.*

In the letters the discussion on technical literary matters focuses on Zukofsky's defence of his major poem "A", and his evident irritation at Pound's failure to appreciate it (pp.112-113). But the reader looking for detailed explication will not find it: Zukofsky wanted Pound to take the lead in detailed criticism, and Pound refused: "Certain things can be remedied more or less by procedures known to yr/venbl/frien' but it wd. Even better to remedy them by procedures evolved by L.Z. ipsissimo."

What is interesting is that as early as 1930 Zukofsky perceived the basic shape of a poem which he did not finish until 44 years later:

> *Yes, as far as I'm concerned right now "A" will be <a> life-work. I don't see how else, if it's going to be 2 movements a summer and 17 more to go to complete the "epic" 24!*

That it was a life-work, Pound disagreed. He thought the poem at that stage ("A" 1-7) needed a "top dressing" of influences removed. He also repeatedly criticised what he saw as a lack of lucidity in Zukofsky's style, and a too literal conception of the poem as a standard musical form in words. Yet by 1936 he wrote that he had enjoyed reading "A"-8, and when Zukofsky visited Pound in St Elizabeth's hospital in 1954 and presented him with a copy of the sequence Anew, Pound wrote to him that he thought Zukofsky had shaken off the influences of Eliot and Pound himself at last, and though "Zuk. On his own. Not ALWAYS comprehensible" nonetheless "damn all I think yu have got yr/ own idiom/".

Certainly he had, and one that was profoundly to influence Creeley among others. But the men who met in 1954 were not the regular correspondents of twenty years earlier. The exchange of letters had been forcibly stopped during the war years never really to pick up again; and prior to its cessation in 1940 the dialogue had become dominated by Pound's attitudes to race and economics.

As the Thirties progressed Zukofsky, despite occasional racial insults from Pound, tried to argue rationally on economics. In 1936 he wrote:

> *"Jewish internationalism" – there ain't no such thing & exists only in yr. mind tainted by Nazi bigotry – or some other infernal silliness beyond yr. sensible control. Might as well speak of Italian internationalism or French or whatever. Bankers inter- nationalism is another matter – but that ain't confined to nations or dispersed nations: that exists, & that's what you want to wipe out.*

Yet two years later, in a letter dated according to the Fascist calendar, Pound was asking Zukofsky if he would accept, along with Bunting, the dedication of Guide to Kulchur. Zukofsky told him if he wanted to dedicate his book to "a communist (me) and a British-conservative-antifascist-imperialist (Basil)" he could go ahead. A year later again and Zukofsky was reduced to asking Pound to drop politics altogether from his letters. But his basic loyalty to Pound he made clear:

...there is no use, the way I'm made up, reasoning with your convictions as they are now. If I'm good enough, I'll reach more fruitful ground. In your case, the best I can do is shut up. That does not mean I don't respect yr. integrity. I've gone on respecting it ever since you got yourself drowned in the batter of credit economics – at a loss <to myself> of every practical & helpful contact in U.S. & Europe. I don't regret it. From point of practical politics, I'm not ready and never will be to attack you before the public. Can't help it, if I start with a feeling like integrity. There are some things that are personal, & one can't build right, on them, as if they were not.

...I cannot see – tho I have made every attempt to understand social credit – that any good can come out of thinking that involves itself in a mess of "incarnation" etc such as Douglas has recently involved himself...

I enclose the first two stanzas of a canzone – knowing what you know about poetry is more than most of us know I'm not ashamed to send you uncompleted work, if you care to be bothered. The local small fry would no doubt accuse me of being a fascist for having lived with the Guido as basis day in & day out for the last two years. You will probably see how far gone I am on the Marx side of it, & attribute all my faults to the influence of his unenlightened use of language. But no matter if there's poetry in <it>, you'll still see it, I believe. Some insight a man never loses. – But let's not correspond about politics etc

   As ever,

     Z

As Tytell describes, Zukofsky was only one of many writers who corresponded with or visited Pound after the war: these included Lowell, Olson, Berryman, Robert Duncan, Thornton Wilder, Eliot, Conrad Aiken, Spender, Elizabeth Bishop, Langston Hughes, MacDiarmid, Ginsberg. It was to Ginsberg in Rapallo in 1967 that Pound, after stating his sense of failure regarding the Cantos, added "But the worst mistake I made was that stupid prejudice of anti-semitism. All along that spoiled everything."

Tytell's biography is a creditable achievement: it is occasion- ally a bit "high" in style (as in the description of Rapallo at the start of Part Two) but it reads easily as a whole, has been care- fully and clearly constructed with much new research, and is a useful condensation of, and guide through, a very great many facts. The Pound-Zukofsky anthology on the other hand, is very expensive for its 96 letters with notes, introduction and biographical appendix; but any large library seriously concerned with Pound should have a copy.

There are people who find themselves unable to read Pound's work sympathetically knowing what he believed, wrote, and cam- paigned for – sometimes in the work itself. The reaction of such people is honest, understandable and not at all to be discredited. But there are others antagonistic to the work whose reactions are not so honest. The "gargoyles" as Pound called them in London, those lovers of excessive adjectives and poetry of "boiled oatmeal consistency", have their successors still flourishing today, and the publication of these two books have given the opportunity once more for these sniffily to dismiss the poetry with the life. But the crux of the matter here is to be found, not in the life, but in the appraisal of the work of Pound and others that Zukofsky made in his 1930 essay "American Poetry 1920-1930" (reproduced in Prep- ositions, Rapp & Carroll 1967). Having quoted Pound's "A new cadence means a new idea," Zukofsky writes "The devices of em- phasizing cadence by arrangement of line and typography have been those which clarify and render the meaning of the spoken word specific." Sixty years on this advance in prosody still cannot be countenanced by some; while for others it is one reason they are grateful for Pound's literary achievement.

News for Babylon: The Chatto Book of
Westindian-British Poetry
ed. James Berry. Chatto and Windus. 1984

History of the Voice:
The Development of Nation Language in
Anglophobe Caribbean Poetry
Brathwaite. New Beacon Books. 1984

News for Babylon, subtitled The Chatto Book of Westindian-British Poetry, and edited by James Berry, has recently been published. Some of the poems included have a strong sense of personal presence and performance, for example "Coolman" by Nkemka Asika:

> Clap
> Hi man hi man
> Clap
> Hi man yes man
> Coolman
> Yeah man coolman
> Yes man coolman
> How are you man?
> Coolman
> Today is a good day
> Coolman
> The weather is holding out
> Beautiful, man
> Yes man, coolman
> Man how life treating you?

Coolman
Coolman where are you going, man?
Coolman
You're really hip
Coolman
You aint playin you hip, man
Coolman
Yes man I'm coolman
Jus' coolman
High man kinky man
Moonman weirdman
Drug man, ass-hole man
Coolman
You see man?
For hundreds of years
You're jus' the same way
Jus' coolman
Jus' coolin' it man
Coolman
Cool it man, coolman
Coolman have you seen
That freak-out chick?
Coolman
Over where? Coolman
Over where, man?
Coolman
Over there man
Coolman, that's cool, man
Coolman
Look coolman
Look man coolman

Look I bring you
Some fire coolman
Coolman
I have some fire
For you coolman
Yes man coolman
Look man coolman
Crush bang
Crush Bang
Crush Bang
Badabang bang
Defrost coolman bang
Bye-bye coolman
Poodoo bang pow
Coolman

Another poet besides Asika, all of whose contributions are worth reading, is Benjamin Zephaniah. This is the last ten lines of his 26-line poem, "For Two Years One Time".

The walls they were covered with nude shots of girls
and smoked cigarette butts were treated like pearls.
I saw prison warders beat men till them sick
and then run them off to the hospital quick.
At night when light out cockroach would congregate,
it was easy to hear lonely men masturbate
they would call girlfriends names or try sexing young men
if you don't know prison please don't go my friend.
For two years one time I lived in a cell,
and really I mean it, it was fucking hell.

But arguably the most forcible poem in the anthology is one called "A Stray from the Tribe" by Rudolph Kizerman. It's 184 lines long. Here are three excerpts:

Everytime I see that old-timer intellectual,
smooth, aloof and Black,
the cat, has lost something
and gained something,
lost his necktie
and gained a word;
he frequently says fuck, nowadays,
and wears a dashiki.

The way I remember the cat
is with low cropped hair
and his moustache blocked; n
ow, he waywardly wears jeans
and digs his share of pot.

Can't see his head
for the hair on top;
for him the really massive Afro is in;
his chicks are not so white anymore.

                    *

The old-timer
has definitely shopped
his superficial intellectuality,
borrowed rhetoric,
refined pauses,

and his obsequious expositions
of elegant irrelevance
in the Great Tradition.

We know
how tough
it's been for the brother;
we know
the quality of shit
and the quantity
he had to balm
his mind in.
We know
What went on.

His academic mentors,
with whom he was in tight league,
filled his pockets
with the fodder
for important degrees...

                    *

Anyway,
now, he turned on
to the familiar Black scenes;
he switches on
such hip jive
you'd hardly believe:
cool it,
swing it,

groove it,
dig it,
screw it,
knock it,
rip off,
pig,
motherfucker,
right on,
keep yer cool,
don't blow yer gig,
don't blow yer stack,
do yer thing,
shit, baby!
Let the brother be;
the cat's just trying
to find his way
back to the tribe
on a new
word train.

In its entirety, Kizerman's poem is about the political nature of language, and the inauthenticity that can result from a person's being unaware of this political nature. It's also about the political nature of education, and this again is why it should seem more relevant to many Scottish writers than the ubiquitous MacDiarmid-versus-Muir warhorse wheeled out every "Whither Scottish Literature?" sleep-in. For there are many writers in Scotland whose first debt is not to the makers or makkars of any literary tradition, but to the people who made certain specific political achievements which have enabled today's working-class writers to be alive and well and sitting facing a typewriter in 1984: achievements such as the National Health Service, shorter working hours, less crowded council housing, welfare benefits, free libraries, and free education. But the education has had to be evaluated carefully. The carrot has been proffered, that there is a unitary society, with an agreed range of values to be discovered in an agreed body of literature: to wit, "the mainstream", or "the tradition". Some have not been fooled. Some have. "A Stray from the Tribe" is about the latter.

Kizermann's poem takes up six of the seven pages allocated to him. There are 206 pages for 40 poets, making an average of just over five pages per poet. As with most anthologies of race or place that try to pack the names in, there's a deal of contributions which read as if they're there to make up the numbers – school-magazine stuff from the School of Worthy Sentiments. What's disconcerting about News for Babylon is that the editor himself is one of the duds – yet he's given his own work by far the most space. The editor, James Berry, allows himself no less than 28 pages – almost one-seventh of the whole book – and this he puts at the end, as if by way of summation. That, it certainly isn't. Repetition, for instance, does not as with Anika, serve to give a snappy ambiguity between intimacy and menace. In Berry's poem, "Speech for an Alternative Creation", it becomes that dreary literary device, anaphora – so beloved of politicians and others trying to make empty rhetoric sound like vatic inspiration of the spirit:

> Let us recreate all things in own image.
> Let us make a new beginning.
> Let us remove night, dawn, dusk,
> remove black thunder, leave lightning,
> dismiss dark November, leave
> all eyes on noon, that dazzle
> of summer, our white heat of days.

Nor is there much liveliness of shifting register: solemnity tends to be all, as in "On an Afternoon Train from Purley to Victoria, 1955":

Hello, she said and startled me.
Nice day. Nice day I agreed.

I am a Quaker she said and Sunday
I was moved in silence
to speak a poem loudly
for racial brotherhood.

I was thoughtful, then said
what poem came on like that?
                ...
Where are you from? She said.
Jamaica I said.
What part of Africa is Jamaica? She said.
Where Ireland is near Lapland I said.
                ...
So sincere she was beautiful
as people sat down around us.

His dialect poems also have a kind of basic deference, a fatal
folksy tendency to the presentable vignette. They lack gutsiness,
there's too much Respect for Literature in the air. In fact as a whole
Berry's lengthy contribution really is a serious error of judgment.
The book's cover proclaims the anthology as "a landmark in Brit-
ish poetry", and Berry himself writes that it "releases a people's
voice with its anguishes, its struggles and its celebrations." Not
true. It's a marketing package, a pretty safe anthology that happens
to include some good, not-very-safe-at-all poets. Unfortunately it
doesn't contain nearly enough of them.

Edward Kamu Brathwaite's History of the Voice, subtitled The
Development of Nation Language in Anglophone Caribbean Po-
etry, is a marketing package of a more academic type, being the
transcript of a lecture given to students at Harvard University in
1979. The lecture is on twentieth-century West Indian poetry writ-

ten in varieties of English, and "nation language" is the term used to cover the present range of language-usage:

—from Linton Kwesi Johnson:

the people demma fite
fe work dung deh
de people dem a fite
one annaddda dung deh

de people demma fite
fe stay alive dung deh
de people demma fite
fe dem rites dung deh

—to Anthony McNeill:

Strange my writing to you
Can I say a cliché
Never thought I would see the day when you would cut
me glimpsed you in should have said at should
have said near a bank one day; smiled; waved; and
you cut me
Catherine name from the north

The appeal of the phrase "nation language" isn't difficult to understand. It does tend to be the same old quarrelling ghosts that haunt the larochs of empire, asking whether it's valid for the local writers to write in a standard English, or whether the albeit-angli-fied local language retains a unique character best presented in a "non-standard" syntax; whether dialect is retrogressive and nar-row, or uncompromising and authentic; whether the pre-colonial culture should be given primacy, or whether it should be given only that respect due to the honourable dead. It's all about ideological status; variants of the de facto language of a nation, versus deviants of the language of the old colonial power. Such arguments always probe that tender spot, which writers should be taken "seriously". The "authority" card then has to be played, and Brathwaite is honest enough not to deal it from the bottom:

> ...I should tell you that the reason I have to talk so much is that there has been very little written on the subject. I bring to you the notion of nation language but I can refer you to very little literature, to very few resources. I cannot refer to what you call an "establishment". I cannot really refer you to Authorities because there aren't any. One of our most urgent tasks is now to create our own Authorities.

But what would actually constitute the status of those "Authorities" which would decide the status of the writings? Which is to say, what does the word "our" mean in "our own Authorities"? For Brathwaite, it probably means "we Carib- beans"; again though, as he gave the lecture at Harvard, maybe it means "we Blacks" or "we Blacks at university". My own difficulty is that as a resident of Great Britain, I tend to think of an "authority" as being someone who has a five-figure salary talking about someone who hasn't. So when I've been through the doors marked "race" and the doors marked "sex", I still tend to get very suspicious if I don't see a door marked "class". But for Brathwaite, class isn't a relevant issue in the development of nation-language poetry in the Caribbean. Maybe that's why I tend to find the quoted poems scattered through this 45-page transcript more interesting than what's said about them. The extensive additional bibliography and discography is what makes the book worth buying.

Kathy Galloway: Love Burning Deep
Poems and Lyrics. SPCK. 1993

A book with such a title and publisher is unlikely to attract those uninterested in exclusively Christian publications, especially if wary of exposure to proselytising. But though there are religious songs and poems in this first collection of Kathy Galloway's that will, I presume, be of most interest to those who share her religious beliefs, there is much that is "simply" about being a human being in the world, and one specific person's attempt to report on that. In her preface she writes, "The metaphors of my inner landscape are those of Christian faith as experienced by me in my context of gender (female) culture (Scottish) and calling (encouragement). But I hope they are not exclusive. They are not meant to be so...one of the things I have found to be true to my experience is that the personal is also political... So my experiences may have echoes in others, and may encourage their exploring." The back cover states that she is a minister of the Church of Scotland, editor of the Iona Community magazine Coracle. The title poem has relevance to a problem that can confront the feminist trying to come to terms with a monotheistic religion which refers to God the "Father". This can suggest that masculinity is somehow eternal and in its perfect ideal state is omnipotent, omniscient, and doesn't need the Female to exist. The Female becomes something that "He" decided to create. If one believes in a personal God, how is this possible to be a "person" in any meaningful way without being either male or female? The song "Love Burning Deep" in fact refers to God as feminine, and speaks of "the shelter of her hand"; another lyric "I cannot call you Lord" states:

I cannot find the word
To fit this woman's hour
That lets me praise the power of love
Not fear the love of power.

But Christ himself is still addressed as "Lord" in this song, one of his attributes being "liberator of the poor". Here be Liberation Theology one might think, and the Nicaraguan priest-poet, Ernesto Cardenal, could come to mind. At least as relevant though would be the work of Latin American women poets after Cardenal – the anthology Lovers and Comrades published by the Women's Press is one source – who express need for liberation not from America or the IMF, but from gender roles within the revolutionary movement. But as a woman minister Kathy Galloway's work uniquely still falls within the remit of theology. It seems that within the context of these poems, Christ is taken as the exemplum of the freedom to be a person, a person even beyond bogus patriarchal limitations. This is the conclusion to "Jesus is nailed to the cross", part of a remarkable Stations of the Cross sequence that climaxes this book:

You cannot criticize the church.
You cannot undermine the state.
You cannot challenge the establishment
and expect benign approval.

Above all.
Let me hammer home the point...
You must not threaten or subvert the patriarchy.
Nor side-step altogether the balance of powers.
How dare you be so impertinently alive?

That is to threaten God,
and we do not like that. Not at all.

So here you go.
Up against the wall.
Bang! Bang! Bang!

Another poem in this sequence, "Women of Jerusalem weep for Jesus" can be seen not only in feminist terms but more generally as a critique of the domestication of images of suffering, television "famine pornography" and the like. The tears disgust, they are "so facile, maudlin, and always on display":

Your acts are needed now, there has been too much of women weeping
Dry your tears, resolve instead by your decision
that there will be in future fewer times
for grief like this.

Or, if you will not put your strength and courage
at the service of resistance to the powers,
then weep for your own children, for your daughters'
daughters.
For, in truth, you will yet live to see them
crushed beneath the weight of mountains, hidden by the hills.

A poem "Gestalt of Intimacy" weighs the love offered by an exclusive intimate relationship against the love in walking out into the "dark shadows" of the world of human needs. It dramatises a moment of choosing the latter. Once you have chosen who you are, another poem puts it, you are free:

Therefore, you may be exactly who you are.
You have inhabited yourself,
you are at home,
and home is where you are,
even if it is the desert.
No-one can dispossess you of your own in-dwelling.
This is what it means to be free.

Not therefore the domestic hearth, as one of the songs puts it: "There are more ways than firesides to keep warm". This stimulating and technically supple collection deserves wide notice.

Norman MacCaig: Collected Poems
Chatto & Windus: The Hogarth Press. 1985

There are 625 poems in this book. Almost all are in the present tense. Most also use the first person, at least in part – some- times to make a concluding observation. Of course the use of the first person in writing does not mean that this person represents the author; but here it seems that it does. The tone and register are constant, the reminiscence sometimes personal to the extent of naming names. There is a deal of quizzical metaphysical teasing of the world-within-world variety – a kind of wink behind the sigh behind the smile. The book is full of animals, fish, landscapes of the Highlands and of Edinburgh, people seen in groups, people seen individually. Often the effect is of a sketch being built up – but always the sketcher himself is present, drawing a moral, making an aside, or asking you to construct a whole from the sequence of constituent parts; you may feel then that you are in the presence of a highly original quick-sketch artist with a copy of Henryson in one pocket and the Metaphysical Poets in the other. Capturing animal movement in shorthand is one of MacCaig's strong points. This, from "Starling on a Green Lawn":

> He makes such a business of going somewhere
> he's like a hopping with a bird in it.

> The somewhere's any place, which he recognises at once.
> His track is zig-zag -zag.

Or this, from "Toad":

Stop looking like a purse. How could a purse
squeeze under the rickety door and sit,
full of satisfaction, in a man's house?

You clamber towards me on your four corners –
right hand, left foot, left hand, right foot.

Or this, from the previously uncollected (there are 115 such poems) "Early Sunday Morning, Edinburgh":

And, fore and hindpaws out of line,
An old dog mooches by, his gold
Eyes hung down below hunched shoulders,
His tail switching, feathery, finely.

("An" is misprinted "And" in the book.) Or this observation of shared shape and movement, from "Things in their elements":

Ten thousand starlings in the air
Right-turn as one, as one go soaring.
A pear-shaped shoal of baby herring
In shallow water do the same.

Or, from "Kingfisher":

That kingfisher jewelling upstream
seems to leave a streak of itself behind it
in the bright air. The trees
are all the better for its passing.

What a rotten verse this would have been, had it started with a definite article rather than a demonstrative pronoun. The demonstrative puts MacCaig "there", pointing at the kingfisher – so the conceit of a retinal after-image, as in a too-slow camera shot , can carry because it is as much an image of MacCaig's surprise as it is of the kingfisher's flight: it is an image of MacCaig's perception of that flight. When people talk, as they do, of MacCaig's "surprising" metaphors and conceits, they do not, in the opinion of this reviewer, note often enough that the metaphors and conceits are images of MacCaig's perception of objects, not images of the objects themselves. This can be seen at work in the last verse of the poem "Small Lochs":

> I know they're just H20 in a hollow.
> Yet not much time passes without me thinking of them.
> Dandling lilies and talking sleepily
> And standing huge mountains on their watery heads.

The "talking sleepily" recalls the closing lines of Henley's "Attadale West Highlands" – a 14-line recollection of Loch Carron:

> Round the shingled shore
> Yellow with weed, there wandered vague and clear
> Strange vowels, mysterious gutturals, idly heard.

Henley's poem also puts in another way the image in MacCaig's last line. The Henley is too long to quote here – but it is worth reading, for its own sake as an attractive if postcardish little portrait; and as a contrast to MacCaig's handling of the same images – both in "Small Lochs" and in "Loch Sionascaig".

Another quite instructive comparison is between MacCaig's short sequence of three-line snowscenes, "Notes on a Winter Journey", and a footnote, and Robert Bly's short sequence of three-line snowscenes, "Snowfall in the afternoon", to be found in that American poet's collection Silence in the Snowy Fields.

This is Bly's third poem in that sequence:

As the snow grows heavy, the cornstalks fade further away,
And the barn moves nearer to the house
The barn moves all alone in the growing storm.

This is MacCaig's third, describing a road far from the city:

So few cars, they leave the snow.
I think of the horrible marzipan
in the streets of Edinburgh.

Comparison with the Bly sequence emphasises the harshness of the MacCaig, an appropriate harshness, as it deals with a winter journey to what proves unexpectedly to be the scene of a close friend's death. This friend is named, as are other friends in happier poems.

It's here that the most fruitful comparative study might be made – that between MacCaig's presentation of the self and that in the poetry of his fellow Apocalyptic poet, WS Graham. Both Graham and MacCaig began as poets whose evident talents still managed to blink intermittently through a turgid porridge of sub-Dylan Thomas, prolix imagery. Both Graham and MacCaig have fought their way to their own voice and, in their older years, have written about the sense of loss at being separated from a friend (Graham's "A Private Poem to Norman MacLeod" and "Dear Bryan Winter"). The fundamental difference between Graham and MacCaig though is in the terms on which they address the reader – in the definition of the self that they choose to employ.

Graham, like MacCaig, uses the first person. Again, that first person refers to the author himself – in Graham's case with his memories of Greenock, his real-life friends, his present environment of Madron, in Cornwall. But Graham is a contemporary of Beckett in a way that MacCaig is not – he addresses the reader directly as he makes his poems, the self-presented is of one struggling to define the relationship between himself and his reader in the very act of writing. He makes metaphor of the physical characteristics, the marks on the page, that "lie between" himself and his audience. This is not some "pose" on Graham's part, or another voyage up a cul-de-sac of writing about writing. It is an awareness on Graham's part of what can and what cannot be assumed about the act of language, least of all about writing the word "I" and expecting all readers to take that as some kind of given, a bone that will only be gnawed at by adolescents and philosophers. In writing, the word "I" is a literary device; Graham brings a great quality of attentiveness to his poems, by being fully aware of that fact yet insisting on seeking ways of tracking down the "I" that will be authentically his own, and will speak directly to the reader on the basis of their relationship as it actually is.

MacCaig's "I" is different, of a different linguistic nature altogether. It refers to an author being beyond the poems, "out of reach" of the reader. The reader enters imaginatively into a relationship with this author, by drawing various selves, in a "dramatic present". But to the self of the author remains the same, intact, impregnable, not becoming another self through dissolution into language.

With the self of the author's therefore you can on occasion agree or disagree. He eschews politics and economics, but his opinions about "progress", for instance, do tend to be rather negative in a generalised way; a poem about phoney rhetoric such as "Smuggler" too, with its distrust of the person who uses words like "justice, fraternity, internationalism, peace, peace, peace" – is a bit easy in itself, some might think.

But there are after all 625 poems to choose from – and of course anyone with any interest whatever in contemporary Scottish writing should read the book. It presents poems from and including Riding Lights of 1955, when MacCaig was already 45 years old. Younger writers hoping not to have petered out by middle age may find that a sobering thought.

The Lord Chamberlain's Blue Pencil
John Johnston: Hodder & Stoughton. 1990

It is just over twenty years since every play to be performed in a public theatre in Britain had first to be approved by the Lord Chamberlain, supervisor of state funerals and weddings, royal investitures and garden parties, receptions for visiting heads of state – and who usually had had some experience in governing a province of India. To do the main work of vetting the thou- sands of scripts required by law to be sent him, examiners or
"readers" were appointed under a comptroller and his assistants – usually army officer class – who reported directly to the Lord Chamberlain himself. The Lord Chamberlain's Blue Pencil is an anecdotal history of theatrical censorship in Britain mainly from the passing of the Theatres Act of 1843. The book is written by a former comptroller, is dedicated to his former colleagues, and uses records not available to the general public.

The 1843 Act allowed the Lord Chamberlain to refuse forever a play's performance "whenever he shall be of opinion that it is fitting for the preservation of good manners, decorum, or the public peace to do so." No reason had to be given, the scripts did not have to be returned, and a charge was levied for the privilege of their compulsory inspection. Any play critical of the institutions of state, or which howsoever represented on stage Royalty, God, politicians, or any living person, was not approved. Victoria, George V, Edward V11, all at intervals made clear their approval of specific acts of censorship, and their desire that this power of censorship remain. "No more parsons in burlesques" came the instruction after one complaint from the Prince of Wales in 1893. Shelley's The Cenci -"all one long horror" according to an examiner this century – finally got its licence a hundred years after it was written. Mrs Warren's Profession, presently at the Citizens, had to wait a more modest twenty-five. The chief examiner was, according to

Johnstone, "the lynchpin" of the system. George Bernard Shaw had this to say of one such examiner E.F.S Piggott, whose "kindly blue pencil" had been dutifully praised in the Press:

> The late Mr Piggott is declared on all hands to have been the best reader of plays we have ever had; and yet he was a walking compendium of vulgar insular prejudice, who, after wallowing all his life in the cheapest theatrical sentiment, had at last brought himself to a pitch of incompetence...He had French immorality on the brain; he had American indecency on the brain; he had the Divorce Court on the brain; he had "not before a mixed audience" on the brain; his official career in relation to the higher drama was one long folly and panic...

It is a frightful thing to see the greatest thinkers, poets, and authors of modern Europe – men like Ibsen, Wagner, Tolstoi, and the leaders of our own literature – delivered helpless into the vulgar hands of such a noodle as this amiable old gentleman – this despised and incapable old official – most notoriously was. The minuted deliberations of the Lord Chamberlain and his advisors must sometimes have seemed like a fine example of the kind of dialogue that they met to suppress. A conference at St James's Palace was addressed on how the theatre "should be maintained on a decent level of propriety" during the Second World War:

> The debate which followed centred around nudity, "objectionable" gags and "business", and the undesirable growth of striptease and bottle parties. A gratifying measure of unanimity was evident and a communiqué was issued summarising the conclusions.

These conclusions were, once again, the need for greater control over "impropriety of gesture and speech" and for the extension of government control to include areas such as cabaret where the Lord Chamberlain's powers did not reach. Johnstone records that "with regard to nudity in revues the Lord Chamber- lain maintained his criterion of allowing only static nude posing." Photographs of all such nude poses in revues had to be sent for inspection. The archives must be prodigious. The Windmill Theatre alone over 32 years accounted for 341 revues containing "nude tableaux". The pose in photographs had to be "artistic", the lighting subdued, the face "expressionless."

There was not always agreement amongst the examiners. Johnstone found himself disagreeing with the examiner Charles Heriot, a graduate of Glasgow University, over a sketch sent in from that same institution's student union:

> I found that I usually agreed with Heriot's recommendations as to whether or not a play should be licensed. One exception was Duel at Durango, a sketch by Alan Steel submitted by Glasgow University Union in 1967. The story was about the planning of a revolution in a South American country where the idea was to assassinate the President and his wife by an explosive contraceptive. Charles Heriot did not recommend a licence because of the nature of the plot and I minuted to the Lord Chamberlain, "I have read the play and I think it is harmless enough to be licensed as it stands." The Lord Chamberlain replied, "I would not fuss about this light bit of nonsense and agree with the Assistant Comptroller."

But many could not be treated so "lightly". Between 1912 and 1968, 723 plays were refused a licence, either outright or because the playwright refused to accept the suggested cuts. This whether or not the plays had been performed in another country, no matter how many times. An unspecified and perhaps unquantifiable number of plays only made it to the boards after cuts and alterations.

The daily grind of excision seems to have been taken up with language taboos. In 1961 Lord Cobbold wrote to someone who had complained that he wasn't visibly strict enough, "You would be surprised to know how much we cut out in words." As he put it in an interview four years later, "Words and phrases rarely cause a lot of difficulty. There are some that we always cut."

Attitudes towards homosexuality form a whole chapter in themselves. Arthur Miller's A View from the Bridge was amongst the many plays censored when they reached Britain; others from home and abroad that mentioned the subject were simply banned altogether. One playscript sent in during 1940 told the story of two men meeting again years after they had had an affair at school; one of the men was now engaged to be married. The script received the response, "His Lordship considers it a piece of impertinence that such a play should have been submitted." In the 1950s Lord Scarborough wrote of Ronald Duncan's play-script The Catalyst that though he thought it had great interest and could be a real success, he was still "not prepared to pick and choose between the good and the bad plays that deal with the subject of homosexuality and lesbianism."

But the ultimate forbidden area – which tended towards Infinity, as it were – was the stage direction "improvisation". Nothing could be licensed that allowed actors freedom to choose what to do on a stage without prior permission for every word and every precisely indicated "business". Staff from the Lord Chamberlain's office were sent to see that plays, once licensed, stuck to the script as passed.

The end came because television drama and subsidised theatre drew attention to a theatre censorship that had preferred to work with commercial theatre managers unnoticed. Repeated public rows reflected badly on the institutions which the system had been designed to protect; on balance it became better for the image of these institutions that the 1843 act be scrapped. So scrapped it was, amongst much talk of "free speech", in 1968.

This clearly written book supplements works such as Richard Findlater's *Banned!* of 1967. Its carefully spilled beans – selected to give "a light touch" according to the author – are often very funny, though not always deliberately so. Its principal value lies in its giving a glimpse from the inside of the structures of censorship in Britain, and the attitudes and beliefs of the people involved in their maintenance.

Furtwängler
Hans-Hubert Schönzeler. Duckworth.1990

At the end of November 1935 Wilhelm Furtwängler toured Britain with the Berlin Philharmonic Orchestra. The Glasgow Heralds of the time show that he did not come to Glasgow on this particular tour, though he conducted a Saturday afternoon concert in Edinburgh. His absence from Glasgow's St Andrew's Halls may not have been regretted a great deal: there was so much going on there in any case. On Saturday, November 23rd the Scottish Orchestra under its then resident conductor John Barbirolli performed Berlioz's Fantastic Symphony. On the Tuesday there was a choral and orchestral concert amongst whose soloists was Heddle Nash. On Thursday 28th, a solo recital by Elizabeth Schumann. On the Friday, a recital by Richard Tauber. On Saturday 30th, Barbirolli and the orchestra were joined by the Russian bass Alexander Kipnis. On these last three nights of November 1935 then, appeared in Glasgow three of the finest classical singers of the century. But each of these singers fled Nazi rule in Germany or Austria. Wilhelm Furtwängler remained. That he did so has never wholly been forgiven by many even of his admirers as a musician. This new biography is another attempt to justify his decision.

The biographies of controversial figures are notoriously difficult to write whilst surviving immediate relatives remain in possession of letters and other material. The biographer with the least pejorative approach is likely to be given the most help. In his preface Schönzeler writes that he is grateful to have been given the chance to write the biography of a man whom he "admired and adored".

Adoration is unfortunately the sustaining tone of the book. One photograph, for instance, shows the conductor's body, head propped on pillows, with a caption supplied by Furtwängler's widow Elizabeth: "This photo was taken one or two hours after he died, still on his death bed, in one of his rehearsal shirts, his hands as I placed them. Truly: Death and Transfiguration." Another photograph shows Furtwängler sitting with his first wife Zitla, who looks an agreeable and pleasant enough person. In the text however she is dismissed in a few lines:

> 'She appears to have been witty, vivacious and elegant, but these appearances were deceptive, for she had no real brains. It is not surprising therefore, that the marriage (which remained childless) was not successful, for the highly cultured Furtwängler only liked the company of people with whom he could discuss music, philosophy and art.'

Not so dismissed is Elizabeth herself, who became Furtwängler's second wife in 1943:

> 'I sometimes wonder whether Furtwängler ever fully realised, or appreciated, what a gem of a woman he had married. She was everything many men dream of as a wife, though not every man finds the fulfilment of that dream: a lover, a mother, a house-wife and – dare I say it? – a nurse-maid at the same time.'

The trouble with this level of banality and one-sidedness is that it makes evaluation impossible when applied to the really important matter of Furtwängler's biography – the extent to which he collaborated with Hitler's regime. Far from clearing the air this short biography – only 122 pages actually relating the sequence of the life – muddies the atmosphere with character assassination of all who dared criticise, let alone oppose, the subject. Those for instance who saw it as "yet another black mark against him" that Furtwängler was photographed shaking hands with Hitler (a photograph not included) apparently have ignored that it was Hitler who shoved his hand in Furtwängler's, not the other way round. Those non-Jews who chose to leave Germany should not perhaps be given unqualified credit. Furtwängler after all "must have known very well that he could have built up an easy life for himself by emigrating". As for the other:

'We must not forget that of all the artists who left Germany between 1933 and 1939 (and after 1938 also Austria and the other territories annexed by Hitler) the vast majority left for racial reasons. It may be cruel to say this, but for them it was relatively easy to come to a decision.'

What a chilling phrase, "for racial reasons". Yet if Schönzeler is unfortunate in his choice of words defending Furtwängler against criticism, he is often no less so when supposedly showing the positive side of Furtwängler's behaviour. Pointing out for instance Furtwängler's defence of Hindemith against Nazi criticism in 1934, Schönzeler notes that Furtwängler "stressed that, apart from being of pure German stock, Hindemith's compositions of the last few years were marked by a true German spirit". Again it is unfortunate that Furtwängler's Beethoven performances of 1942 and 1943 should be described thus:

'...if we listen to the live recordings of these concerts we are astounded by the positive and optimistic utterance, the strength transcending all mundane circumstances, with which Furtwängler could raise the "Ode to Joy" in the Ninth and the glorious apotheosis of victory in the C Major Finale of the Fifth to such Olympian heights... Those who were present at the performances must have understood the wordless message which he conveyed by the music.'

From the language here one might be forgiven in thinking that the message was Strength Through Joy. According to Schönzeler, the optimism would have been understood as anticipation of the defeat of Nazism. Perhaps. Yet the fact that there was no music by Jewish composers in any Furtwängler programme since he last "dared" play a little Mendelssohn in 1934 would not have clarified the matter.

Furtwängler was not himself a Nazi, and he did use influence to help save some musicians. He was a great conductor who's final 1952 Eroica recording would always be in my own "Desert Island" selection. But Furtwängler's wartime performances of Beethoven are another matter. Then it was not simply Beethoven being performed, it was not-Mendelssohn, not-Mahler, not-Jewish-music. I have never felt free to listen to these recordings, and it would take a better biography than this to make me reconsider.

Tony Benn: Diaries 1977-80
Ed: Ruth Winstone. Hutchinson. 1990

Denis Healey: When Shrimps Learn to Whistle
Michael Joseph. 1991

This is the fourth volume of Tony Benn's political record of what he heard, saw and said in Cabinet, Party Conference and else- where, with his passing opinions thereon. A feature is his repeated frustra- tion that the government of which he is a member should adopt policies which, as his own introduction puts it, came later to be known as "Thatcherism": – "Full employment is no longer on the agenda of a Labour Government. They haven't even got a strategy for the eighties. They simply haven't got a strategy." (8/3/77); "... there were we abandoning basic socialist principles while the band prepared for the Queen's Jubilee." (21/5/77); "... it is true that we are pursuing absolutely Tory policies and it is not surprising that the IMF like it or that the Labour movement should be getting restive." (14/12/77); "This is the death of the Labour Party. It be- lieves in nothing anymore, except staying in power." (15/1/78)

Of the prospect of militancy being blamed for impending elec- toral defeat in 1979 he wrote: "...the reality is that we've had a right-wing Leader, a right-wing Cabinet, a right-wing manifesto and a right-wing campaign." (2/5/79) "I wouldn't worry about revolutionary socialism. I don't suppose there are half a dozen rev- olutionaries in London. There isn't a Labour Party – it's dead – and nobody has thought about socialism in this House for years." (20/5/80)

On oil revenues: "We are not putting it into capital expenditure or public investment of one kind or another; we are going to give it away in tax cuts: that is the measure of the Labour Government." (16/2/78) On "the sale of the century", the sale of BP: "We have provided a blueprint for selling off public assets in the future and we will have no argument against it. It is an outrage." (24/6/77) On Gerard Kaufman and closures in British Steel: "- the butcher, on behalf of the Government, of another great industry." (11/12/78) On going to visit a protest about closures in Corby, with its 72% Scottish workforce: "I couldn't tell them, but the Labour Cabinet had decided in February this year to support the closure of Corby. The guys are now faced with the prospect of 30 per cent male unemployment, and they have called in the Labour Party to help them fight. An awful irony; I felt terribly guilty." (11/9/76)

Of his colleagues: "When you get the so-called left of the Party so far to the right, then does it mean there is no support in the country for radical views?" Some of the quotes from others ought to be written on their tombstones. Joel Barnett, to be made a peer of the realm in 1983, had this to say of proposed wage rises for Health Service workers: "...the trade union leaders have raised the expectations of people on £60 a week, who do not starve, and anyway 50 per cent of their wives are at work." (1/2/79) Roy Mason, Northern Ireland minister, when told that rising unemployment might cause civil unrest in Britain, replied: "Male unemployment in Northern Ireland is almost 30 per cent, and there is no trouble there." (6/7/78)

Throughout, he was hoping to make party policy more directly responsible to annual conference. Government policy, on the other hand, seemed not even to be in the control of the Government: "The Treasury doesn't want to upset the IMF, and the FO doesn't want to upset the EEC, and the Ministry of Defence doesn't want to upset Nato." (25/8/77) Pleasing the IMF led to what he came to call "the old Thatcher/Healey view on spending" (12/9/79) – "All this monetarist stuff is, in my view, absolute rubbish." He argued for protectionism against monetarism in the Cabinet on October 7th, 1976, included in his previous volume Against the Tide. The previous December to that – Tuesday 9th – Healey had come to the Cabinet and said "We must get £3.75 billion cuts for 1977-78." By October 1977 Healey "for a disastrous policy" sat in Cabinet "radiating the approval of the world bankers."

Healey thirteen years later has some absorbing tales to tell about banking in his new selection of articles and speeches dating from 1947 until May of this year. The book takes its title from Khrushchev's statement that the Soviet Union would give up Marx, Engels and Lenin only "when shrimps learn to whistle." Healey writes that "The future is now impossible to predict," and that advances in information technology "have made a nonsense of the old economic rules." The "globalisation" of computerised share marketing, deregulation, and "the invention of new financial instruments for hedging risk" now means that "nobody now knows where the risk lies if anything goes wrong." He says that it was reckoned in 1985 that 50 thousand billion dollars annually crossed the exchanges "in search of profit" as distinct from 2 thousand billion "to finance world trade." This former figure Healey reckoned three years later to have doubled to a hundred thousand billion.

There is instability caused by the strain of current world debts. An 80% increase in Third World debt, he says, has been caused specifically by conditions laid down by the industrial world and OPEC; eight hundred billion dollars have become irrecoverable in loans to the Third World from private banks. And America itself (May 1990) "has now got a very fragile financial system" – bailing out their Savings Banks alone is likely to cost "up to five hundred billion dollars." If he were the patriotic citizen of a poor Latin American country he writes, "I would be training youngsters of eighteen or nineteen to plant computer viruses in the banking systems in New York and then threaten to let rip unless the banks made a better deal than they are prepared to so far." Perhaps Tony Benn should have advised him to do the same to the IMF.

Then there is the new political instability to be feared from what Healey calls the "Balkanisation" of post-Gorbachev Europe. An "anarchy" of nation-states he says is an anachronism in a world with nuclear weapons. A new "world order" no less is needed, and he goes into some suggestions using the new Europe and the United Nations as the models. Then, having finished his twenty-four pieces, together with signposts for a new world order, Healey sent the book to the publishers, who sent it to the printers. And then Iraq annexed Kuwait.

Some bits might still be useful here. In 1959 Healey wrote that Britain "...has a unique financial interest in the existing system by which Middle Eastern oil is produced and marketed. This special national interest is most dramatically illustrated by the stupendous contribution made by Kuwait to the dollar reserves of the sterling area and to the investment funds of the London capital market." It was the threat of withdrawal of funds from Britain by Kuwait in 1975, (Benn's diaries, July 1ˢᵗ) that forced a change in Government policy then. Regarding the influence of the debt crisis on the banking system, Healey wrote ten years later in 1985, "...the risk of breakdown is steadily increasing because the strains are becoming intolerable at both ends of the process." By May 1990 he could write, "Most of my American friends in financial institutions think the system would collapse if there were a recession."

In early nineteenth century Europe the newly discovered ruins of ancient Empires were interpreted in two ways. Some saw them as images of past heathen civilisations whose ruination was a vindication of the values of the surviving civilisations of the present. Others including of course many of the Romantics saw them as in fact imaging a reminder and a warning of the future. Amidst all the present daily triumphalism about Eastern Europe, from newspaper ads about "super estates at silly prices" to pseudo-academic tripe about "the death of History", it seems to have been at least realised that Communism is not the only system that is capable of collapse.

The Collected Poems of William Carlos Williams
Volume 1 (1909-1939)
ed. A. Walton Litz & Christopher Magowan
Volume 2 (1939-1962)
ed. Christopher Magowan. Carcanet. 1989

These are the first two volumes of what should be the definitive edition of the collected poetry of William Carlos Williams. They supersede the out of print New Directions/McGibbon & Kee Collected Early Poems, the Collected Later Poems, and Pictures from Brueghel. The next and last volume in the new edition will contain Paterson.

First some statistics. There are 746 titled poems in the two volumes, of which 170 did not appear in the old collections aforementioned. To this additional material is further added 75 translations from other poets, 15 "first versions" of poems subsequently revised, and four works which are a mix of prose and poetry, and from which the previous collections cut out the prose. In the largest of these, the 1923 Spring and All – Williams's first major work after Eliot's "The Waste Land" – the prose takes up half of the work's 60 pages in Volume 1.

These statistics might suggest about a quarter to a fifth of the original work is previously uncollected. It's half that proportion, about 54 out of the 402 pages of original poetry in Volume 1, and 42 out of 408 in Volume 2. That's still a lot, enough for the larger libraries to buy these books even if they have the older collections in stock. Two more reasons are that for the first time the chronology of the work is made clear in the printing. Those who have tried to follow the chronology of the Collected Earlier Poems will know what a difference that makes. That volume had for example the gathering Al Qui Quire (1917) follow An Early Martyr (1935); again, the four poems pages 458-460 for instance, could be dated

1941, 1928, 1933, 1951 – a bit misleading for something titled The Collected Earlier Poems. Williams's development can at last now be followed in the poems as printed. Secondly, there are notes to the poems with significant variants, and – in Volume 1 – some previously unpublished comments by Williams himself. These were transcribed by James Thirlwall when going through the Collected Earlier Poems with the poet Williams in the late 1950's. Thus of poem 24 in Spring and All, the poet is quoted as saying "I was writing in my own language, and whatever the language suggested I wrote. I was following the beat in my own mind, of the American idiom." This connects with another quote from Williams, previously only published in the note to a translation of Sappho published in 1957:

> I'm 73 years old. I've gone on living as I could as a doctor and writing poetry on the side. I practised to get money to live as I please, and what pleases me is to write poetry. I don't speak English, but the American idiom. I don't know how to write anything else, and I refuse to learn.

This idiom was more than just a matter of speech. One of the shorter works that mix prose and poetry, the 1927 A Folded Skyscraper, is in four sections, 1 and 3 being poetry, 2 and 4 prose. Section 4 is a reminiscence of Williams sitting in his smoke-filled car thinking about poetry, about Ezra Pound "opposed with a laugh to my fervent, my fierce anger to have a country." Williams has been out "looking for a number on a house down by Guinea Hill" in other words out on his doctor's rounds. He's debating within himself the difference between his own approach and Pound's going to the Italian renaissance for materials:

> -And while I was thinking all this I seen this gink come running down the hill, on the concrete like a Marathon runner at the first mile, a running by the front of my coupe without looking right nor left, in his cap, and went in at the horse entry of a lot with a kind of fence in front of it where

there was a scrubby stick of a young wild cherry tree all growin' in among the boards – holdin' it up growin' from a pit a bird had – there when the fence was first built – and kept on running down the kind of a dirt road down the middle of the lot where there was only one half the gate made of slats about as high as a man and a couple of trees back in it, a sort of store-lot for a contractor, it looked like, with a lot of things laying around, half rusty on the white grass there was there and a lot of dried weeds sticking in the bottom of the fence....

Down beyond the two-storey shed you could see an old concrete mixer – and right near the slat fence there was a pile of logs about ten feet long and about a foot and a half thick, a lot of junk like that all the way back on both sides of the road with a stack of old boards, a post that had been painted red and with a hawser hole in the top stuck in the ground on one side – Well he kept on running, hopping it along down the ruts under the shed, as I'm telling you, and went on through, past the two trees and everything, a whole row of dumpcarts standing there with the tail boards let down like a two year old's diapers hanging round the knees standing there with a pole shaft stuck in the ground, rusty looking, and there was a kind of rusty boiler like, leaning on a pile of junk back there, an awful heap of stuff in that lot and you could see there was a lot more junk back of the house, you could see it by the concrete mixer I was telling you about.

In other words, as he interjects in "Della Primavera Trasportata al Morale" three years later:

a green truck
dragging a concrete mixer
passes
in the street –
the clatter and true sound
of verse –

Or in other words, as he wrote in "Between Walls" in 1938:

the back wings
of the

hospital where
nothing

will grow lie
cinders

in which shine
the broken

pieces of a green
bottle

Or again it's the "stuff of bushes and small trees" in the much anthologised "By the Road to the Contagious Hospital" from "Spring and All", or the figure 5 in gold on a red firetruck hurtling through the city in the equally well anthologised "The Great Figure".

Williams is to an extent following the advice of the female figure who took him over the city in the early poem "The Wanderer" whose first version, in Volume 1, dates from 1917:

The patch of road between precipitous bramble banks,
The tree in the wind, the white house, the sky!
Speak to them of these concerning me!

Certainly a sizeable proportion of Williams's work describes trees and plants, and scenes that link sky, ground, and the wind; but it's the invocation to rescue the specific from a general context that seems to me important here. This sense of "rescuing" some- thing is often linked to making something with it, as in "To be Hungry is to be Great":

The small, yellow grass-onion
spring's first, green precursor
to Manhattan's pavements, when
plucked as it comes, in bunches,
washed, split and fried in
a pan, though inclined to be
a little slimy, if well cooked
and served hot on rye bread
is to beer a perfect appetizer –
and the best part
of it is they grow everywhere.

This aspect of Williams's work I would call constructivist, if that word hadn't already been grabbed to mean something else in the history of art. Here's another instance of it, in "To a Young Sycamore":

I must tell you
this young tree
whose round and firm trunk
between the wet

pavement and the gutter
(where water
is trickling) rises
bodily

into the air with
one undulant
thrust half its height –
and then

dividing and waning
sending out

young branches on
all sides –

hung with cocoons –
it thins
till nothing is left
but two

eccentric knotted
twigs
bending forward
hornlike at the top

A quote from Aristotle, of whom Williams approved, is here appropriate:

> '..it is possible, using the same medium, to represent the same subjects in a variety of ways. It may be done partly by narration and partly by the assumption of a character other than one's own, which is Homer's way; or by speaking in one's own person without any such change; or by representing the characters as performing all the actions dramatically.'
> — (Aristotle: Chap 3 of On the Art of Poetry (trs T.S. Dorsch) in *Classical Literary Criticism Penguin* 1965, p.34)

But, Williams insisted, one had to be clear what Aristotle – "misinterpreted for over two thousand years and more" – meant by imitation, and what he didn't:

> 'The objective is not to copy nature and never was, but to imitate nature, which involved active invention, the active work of the imagination... To imitate nature involves the verb to do. To copy is merely to reflect something already there, inertly.'
> — (*Autobiography* New Directions Paperbook 1967 p.241)

Movement over stasis, verb over noun. This is not a turning away from naming, the abandoning of language as a vehicle of common sense, and common experience, reference. Rather it's the perception of described, describer and poem as "a field of energy". One can compare this last-quoted poem "To a Young Sycamore" with Clare's 1835 "The Nightingale's Nest". (In passing, you might also like to compare Williams's "Love Song" beginning "Sweep the house clean" Vol.1 p.79, alongside Herrick's great poem "Corinna's Going a Maying".) This is an excerpt from Clare:

> Ay, as I live! Her secret nest is here,
> Upon this whitethorn stump! I've searched about
> For hours in vain. There! Put that bramble by – Nay, trample on its branches and get near....
> ...How curious is the nest! No other bird
> Uses such loose materials, or weaves
> Its dwelling in such spots: dead oaken leaves
> Are placed without and velvet moss within,
> And little scraps of grass, and – scant and spare,
> Of what seem scarce materials – down and hair; For from
> men's haunts she nothing seems to win.

Clare presents himself as if threading through the woodland bushes, and speaks to the reader as if that reader is a companion with him on his search. It's the "dramatic present", a fiction for the reader to participate in, rooted in the specificness of Clare's clarity of eye, allowing him to present the specificness of a real nightingale's nest in the real world.

Williams to an extent employs the fiction of dramatic personae, if one accepts the "I" and "you" of line one as people supposedly standing on a pavement by a tree. But of course the "you" could simply be the reader in a chair, and the first line the ironic adoption of the register of a quasi-intimate public speaker's prefacing a story his audience might find hard to believe: "This guy comes up and asks for a thousand pounds," etc. The "story" itself has a sense of ambiguity – right to the end there's the possibility of it being simply a tale plus punchline – "There's this tree growing here and it's going to get chopped down." But there's no punch- line, so retrospectively it's established that the articulation of the story is "just" the articulation of the tree's growth.

What is at play here are ambiguities upon the function of the Present Tense. To connect these with the quote from Aristotle, these can be described as the "dramatic present", which involves the use of fictional personae; the "actual present", which requires further differentiation into the actual present that the writer inhabits, and that of the reader reading; and the "universal present", which is that which continually or continuously exists in the physical world inhabited by writer, reader, and artwork. The terms are mine of course, not Aristotle's. So often bad writing consists of using the "dramatic present" – "He leans upon his spade and thinks" – as if it were the universal. Thus writer and reader share an "actual" world that is based on denying full existence to what is merely the emblem of a type, whilst deluding themselves that they are participation at the level of the universal-moral.

Not Williams. Another instance, "To a Poor Old Woman":

munching a plum on
the street a paper bag
of them in her hand

They taste good to her
They taste good
to her. They taste
good to her

You can see it by
the way she gives herself
to the one half
sucked out in her hand

Comforted
a solace of ripe plums

seeming to fill the air
They taste good to her

The sharing is not between reader and writer "about". It is the sharing, by writer and reader, in the articulation of a movement that is in empathetic identification with the movement of the poem's subject. "You can see it" in verse three because the language does it in verse two.

Growing plants and trees, women, art. Brueghel was the artist whom Williams focussed on finally in this aspect of his work, in the great sequence Pictures from Brueghel published in 1962, in Williams's 78th year. He first wrote of Breughel's work in the poem "The Dance" that appeared in the 1944 collection The Wedge:

> In Brueghel's great picture, The Kermess,
> the dancers go round, they go round and
> around, the squeal and the blare and the
> tweedle of bagpipes, a bugle and fiddles
> tipping their bellies (round as the thick-
> sided glasses whose wash they impound)
> their hips and their bellies off balance
> to turn them. Kicking and rolling about
> the Fair Grounds, swinging their butts, those
> shanks must be sound to bear up under such
> rollicking measures, prance as they dance
> in Brueghel's great picture, The Kermess.

In some ways this marks a breaking away from other poems quoted in its relentless internal rhymes and alliterations. But of course these are functional, and the "imitation" aspect is still relevant. The 1962 sequence returns to the sparer building-up style, but there is added the writer's perception of the artist in his work, which is why it is fitting that the sequence begins with the Breughel self-portrait:

In a red winter hat blue
eyes smiling
just the head and shoulders

crowded on the canvas
arms folded one
big ear the right showing

the face slightly tilted
a heavy wool coat
with broad buttons

gathered at the neck reveals
a bulbous nose
but the eyes red-rimmed

from overuse he must have
driven them hard
but the delicate wrists

show him to have been a
man unused to
manual labour unshaved his

blond beard half trimmed
no time for any-
thing but his painting

A cubist portrait of a medieval Flemish painter's self-portrait. Another in the sequence, "Haymaking", harks back in its implications to the itemising prose excerpt quoted earlier from "A Folded Skyscraper":

The living quality of
the man's mind
stands out

and its covert assertions
for art, art, art!
Painting

that the Renaissance
tried to absorb
but

it remained a wheat field
over which the
wind played

men with scythes tumbling
the wheat in
rows

the gleaners already busy
it was his own –
magpies

the patient horses no one
could take that
from him

Williams's identification with Brueghel here is obvious. Some-times that celebration of himself as artist can seem too overt if one is reading these books in large amounts at a time: on occasions I felt like stealing away and leaving him to it. Another trait some might get bored with is Williams's generalisations upon gender, the "male and female of it". As he says in his autobiography, women gave him the energy in his life, a few men the direction. The poem being a field of energy, not direction, this identification between women, flowers and plants, art, plus the artist William Carlos Williams and selected other artists – this can get to be a bit exclusive. One other negative aspect, to do with the printing rather than the poems, is that the addition of new material has been at the expense of some space to let the poems breathe. The old editions, unlike the new, let half-page poems have the page to themselves. For a writer of Williams's structural principles I have tried to describe here, that can make a significant aesthetic difference.

Nothing should detract though from the recognition that this is a major publishing event, the publication at long last of the complete poetry of William Carlos Williams. In a previous short review of the books I was asked to do for City Limits I tried to draw attention to aspects I haven't even mentioned here, and wrote that "No poet has so emphatically the nineteenth century perception of City as metaphor for an inner emptiness of the human." This is the kind of poem I had in mind:

APPROACH TO A CITY

Getting through with the world –
I never tire of the mystery
of these streets: the three baskets
of dried flowers in the high

barroom window, the gulls wheeling
above the factory, the dirty
snow – the humility of the snow that
silvers everything and is

trampled and lined with use – yet
falls again, the silent birds
on the still wires of the sky, the blur
of wings as they take off

together. The flags in the heavy
air move against a leaden
ground – the snow
pencilled with the stubble of old

weeds: I never tire of these sights
but refresh myself there
always for there is small holiness
to be found in braver things.

ESSAYS

MATER TENEBRARUM:

A study of James Thomson (1834-82),
"Bysshe Vanolis"

> He told me once
> The saddest thing that can befall a soul
> Is when he loses faith in God and Woman;
> For he had lost them both. Lost I those gems - Thought the
> world's throne stood empty in my path, I would go wan-
> dering back into my childhood, Searching for them with
> tears.
> – *Alexander Smith: A Life Drama*

"The City of Dreadful Night" – the most pessimistic poem in the English language – is a poem written by a man, addressed to men, about a state of consciousness, indeed a state of existence, considered peculiarly masculine. It is also a despairing response to Saint Paul's First Epistle to the Corinthians, and to the Book of Revelations. It occupies a logical position in the output of a poet whose work constantly presents a male, guilty in body and in mind, looking for acquittal to a female – be that female a real woman, a dead woman, a celestial woman, a woman from a non-Christian afterlife, sleep seen as female, the muse seen as female, and last (but most certainly not least) oblivion seen as female.

From the outset, James Thomson's poetry shows a basic con-flict: the conflict of a man with a deep sense of Christian guilt and sin, and a weak Christian faith. He was born in Port Glasgow when the place was alight with millenialist sects, and his mother – "mystically inclined" with Edward Irving – held all Protestant as well as Catholic churches to be in error, and the Second Coming to be at hand; as for the poet's father, it was only after a stroke had affected his mind that he began taking his son to private spiritual gatherings, which "were not the sort of things with which he had

anything to do in his days of soundness". In 1842 shortly before the death of his mother, the eight-year-old Thomson was placed in the Royal Caledonian Asylum, London, and reared thence- forth along orthodox Church of Scotland lines, having to learn off by heart the Shorter, then the Longer Catechism. In so doing he must have been obliged to unlearn those aspects of his religious beliefs his new mentors would have considered heretical. By the time Thomson left the Caledonian Asylum in 1850, he would therefore have been consistently grounded in the alleged sinfulness of men, but less consistently grounded in the nature of their alleged salvation. The poetry Thomson subsequently wrote in his ten years as army schoolmaster from 1852, repeatedly describes a male looking to a female to restore his lost religious faith; this position is abandoned in the poetry Thomson wrote after he left the army and was staying with the atheist Charles Bradlaugh. These poems exchange the mariolatrous for more down-to-earth, naturalistic depictions of lower middle class urban courtship. But the transition is not made without some signs of strain, and the poems that Thomson wrote after he left Bradlaugh's home and began living on his own in 1866, show the male still possessed by an intense personal sense of guilt. Neither does the conscious rationalisation of this guilt assuage it. The opening words of "The City of Dreadful Night" show the male confiding to the reader that he, as a writer, has arrived at an ultimate position of self-debasement:
"Lo, thus, as prostrate, 'In the dust'".

The reader following the process in Thomson's poetry will be struck, in the poems he wrote as army schoolmaster, by the number of poems in which a man seems to be talking to an absent or dead girl in his head – a kind of "emotion recollected in insomnia" affair. The reader will also be struck by the banality of much of the verse: but it's worth reading, to follow the progress of the poet's mind. Three poems in this period 1852-62 –
"Love's Dawn", "Bertram to the Most Noble and Beautiful Lady Geraldine", and "The Deliverer" – are examples of poems in which the guilty male shows confidence in the female's powers of redemption. The man in "Love's Dawn" regrets that the woman will see through him to:

My heart's caged lusts the wildest and the fiercest,
The cynic thoughts that fret my homeless mind,
My unbelief, my selfishness, my weakness,
My dismal lack of charity and meekness

But he has confidence in her gaze:

For, amidst all the evil, thou wilt find
Pervading, cleansing, and transmuting me,
A fervent and most holy love for thee.

Similarly, the "torpid and defiled" Bertram finds that after he has met the Lady Geraldine, "Numb Faith re-lives", and he is able to address her as:

Blessed Redeemer of my sinking mind

The male persona of "The Deliverer" is told:

Chastity, purity and holiness
Shall shame thy virile grossness....

Till perfect reverence for her shall grow
to faith in God.

But in other poems written in this decade, the male has less confidence. In "Marriage" he requests that his long-absent wife return to him as:

Strength and hope and faith are waning

And the male in "Tasso to Leonara" tells the female:

You are truer than my faith

And asks for "some dear secret sign" that they will really meet after death.

In "Mater Tenebrarum" the female has died, and the male nightly cries on her to visit him from her "Heaven above" that she might give him:

> One word of solemn assurance and truth that the soul with its love never dies!

But still, contradictorily, he clings on:

What keeps me yet in this life, what spark in my frozen breast?
A fire of dread, a light of hope, kindled, O Love, by thee;
For thy pure and gentle and beautiful soul, it must immortal be.

The truth is though, that the male in Thomson's poetry never shows any belief in a "loving" God in the first place. At worst God is God the Avenger, at best he looks the other way. Unlike the female, he is not inclined to forgive, as this episode from "The Doom of a City" illustrates:

> As one who in the morning shine
> Reels homeward, shameful, wan, adust,
> From orgies wild with fiery wine
> And reckless sin and brutish lust:
> And sees a doorway open wide,
> And then the grand Cathedral space;
> And hurries in to crouch and hide
> His trembling frame, his branded face.
>
> ...How can he join the songs of praise?
> His throat is parched, his brain is wild:
> How dare he seek the Father's gaze,
> Thus hopeless, loveless and defiled?
> How taint the pureness – though he yearn
> To join such fellowship for aye?

He creeps out pale – May he return
Some time when he shall dare to stay!

So it is to the female that the male constantly looks for moral strength and faith – faith in an afterlife which the male, purified of his guilty mind and body at last, can share with the female who has given him the faith entitling him to the afterlife with her in the first place. God himself is to be conspicuous by his absence in this Heaven of Thomson's; having arranged the eternal marriage, God can go and do his avenging somewhere else. Thomson seems to have been trying to construct an afterlife whose real God is Shelley; the tribute to Shelley in the first half of the nomde-plume "Bysshe Vanolis" is not simply a matter of style. But Shelley and a sense of sin do not mix. "Reproach not thine own soul" is hardly the motto of the Longer Catechism. So by the time Thomson left the army to stay with Bradlaugh in 1862, the male persona has been reduced – in "To Our Ladies of Death" – to calling on Our Lady of Oblivion. But even in oblivion, it is hoped there might be some little consciousness:

No sin, no fear, no failure, no excess.

In becoming closely associated with Charles Bradlaugh and his anti-theistic National Reformer, Thomson was not mixing in circles whose criticism of religion was solely confined to disput-ing the truth of the Bible and the existence of God. The Nation-al Reformer attacked the adverse effects of the Christian religion in many areas, including on the status of, and on male attitudes towards, women. And when a regular contributor admitted that "the passion of Love" made him hope to be reunited with his wife after death, he was answered the following week by an editorial comment that he had confused reason with sentiment – and that the widowed who remarried might shrink from the complications of a polygamous afterlife. Not surprisingly, the long "Vane's Sto-ry" written between 1862 and 1864, marks a crucial shift in the attitude of the male from that in "Mater Tenebrarum" of 1859.

In "Vane's Story" the male's monologue is set in a frame of defensive irony. Maybe the dead female did visit Vane – and maybe she didn't; maybe the poem is serious – and maybe it's a tall tale.

Between it's satiric prologue and epilogue, the poem proper, 1,205 lines, can be seen as falling into three sections. In the first, Vane tells how his "Rose of Heaven" visited him, and seriously discussed his lack of faith and his belief that Christians are hypocrites; in the second section he recalls how she started laughing at his concern with "old bogey-tales of Hell", and how she told him that Shelley and Heine are alive in the afterlife. Vane then asked her to arrange, through Shelley's intercession, for the early despatch of "Our Lady of Oblivious Death". But in the third section Vane describes how after this lengthy dialogue was concluded, he and his visitor simply went off to a local dance- hall, for an evening's dancing together.

In functional terms, "Vane's Story" quite literally describes the process of the male trying to bring his heavenly female down to earth at last; the way that irony and emotion sit uncomfortably in the poem show though that it's a pretty tricky business. Now that she has arrived, the male is next seen in a series of poems by Thomson describing, in vignettes sometimes quite pleasant, sometimes a bit arch, lower middle-class life couples "stepping out" together. But "The Naked Goddess" of 1867 – written when Thomson had begun living on his own – puts a stop to these. In "The Naked Goddess", the goddess of the title is seen on a hill overlooking a city, and the citizens of the place troop up the hill to marvel at her. Evidently challenged by her nakedness, a preacher offers to save her:

Spirit strangled in the mesh
Of the vile and sinful flesh

Whilst a "sage" offers to bring her:

To full sovereignty of thought
Crowned with reason's glorious crown.

But the clothes offered the goddess by the preacher are so constricting that her body bursts through them, and the gown offered by the philosopher is so baggy she dismisses it as suit- able only for those with a body fit not to see. A little boy and girl whom she welcomes are the only two people in the city to benefit from the encounter; they eventually travel to a distant island where they found a state dedicated to her. The city goes to ruin and "decay" on the other hand as soon as the goddess has departed, and the priest and the philosopher:

Died accursed in sombre rage.

The message of the poem is quite uncompromising: if the spirit of children is not to be "strangled" by telling them their bodies are vile and sinful, or their minds are much more important (being that which raises them above the animal) then to protect them they must be removed from the influence of clergy and intellectual teachers before it is too late. But where does this leave the adult male of Thomson's poems? The answer is to be found in the poem "In the Room" which Thomson wrote the following year: in this allegory the male lying on the bed amongst the chattering furniture is dead – he has taken his own life. Cognition of the malaise – guilt of body and introspection of mind – has not been synonymous with its cure. That the condition affects males rather than females is suggested in the complaint:

The girls are better than these men
Who only for their dull selves care.

As instance of this, the memory of a previous lodger, Lucy, is recalled in a passage of appalling but instructive sentimentality. Lucy apparently had been interested in all the room's objects, dusting and mending; "fifty times a day" the mirror says, she would "smile here on my face", adjusting her hair or tying a ribbon; she had got up early in the mornings, and opened the curtains; she hadn't sat writing all the time, apart from "once a week a pretty note";

nor had she read "those stupid, worn-out books"; she had had her friends, too, "blithe young girls" who had visited her – not like the "glum and sour" man now lying on the bed, who had never had any visitors. Lucy, in short, is another of Victorian Literature's empty-headed dolls. But she is meant to be seen, in comparison with the male in the poem, as cheerful, extrovert, happy with her own appearance, and not a "thinker". But for the man, despair of mind and body has followed despair of spirit, into suicide. The following year, 1969, Thomson wrote virtually no poetry. A diary entry for November 4th records that he spent five hours burning all his old letters and most of his manuscripts:

> Burned all my old papers, manuscripts, and letters, save the book mss, which have been already in great part printed.

> ... after this terrible year, I could do no less than consume the past. I can now better face the future, come in what guise it may.

Two months later, in January 1870, he began work on "The City of Dreadful Night".

The City of Dreadful Night :An Analysis

> "a man in himself is a city, beginning, seeking, achieving
> and concluding his life in ways in which the various aspects
> of a city may embody if imaginatively conceived – any
> city, all the details of which may be made to voice his most
> intimate convictions."
> – W.C.Williams: "Argument" to Book One of *Paterson*

It may seem a paradox, given that the male persona of the po-
ems is now "dead", that the poems – and he – should continue
at all. But this paradox, and this "death", is precisely what "The
City of Dreadful Night" is about. The narrator here, prostrate, tells
the reader that he is writing in the dust something that is not for
the religious, the hopeful, or the successful. Only those who know
the secret already will understand, no "uninitiate" can divine the
meaning of the message. The poem itself, in twenty-one sections,
presents a series of paradoxical images written, like the opening
"Proem", in the present tense.

These images are contained in the even-numbered sections, two
to twenty. On the other hand the odd-numbered sections one to
twenty-one give a series of accounts, in the past tense, of aspects
of a visit to this city made by the narrator himself. These accounts
function both as a guide, literally, to the place itself, and to how
people arrive there. The image contained in the "message", funda-
mentally, is of a city-state, of "Death-in-Life". The only certitude
that the living and sane have there, is "The certitude of Death";
the thing felt least strange is that "Death- in-Life is the eternal
king"; the hopelessness felt is at wonder as to whether Death in
Life can be brought to Life again; the men there are like phantoms;
the sound of traffic is most likely to be the sound of a hearse going
by; the men live in the tombs, the "wan and cold" reason in their
central brain able only to watch their outward madness; people or-

dinarily complain that time passes too quickly, but the time towards death can't pass quickly enough for these citizens:

O length of the intolerable hours,
O nights that are as aeons of slow pain,
O Time, too ample for our ample powers,
O Life, whose woeful vanities remain
Immutable for all of all our legions
Through all the centuries and in all the regions
Not of your speed and variance we complain.

We do not ask a longer term of strife,
Weakness and weariness and nameless woes;
We do not claim renewed and endless life
When this which is our torment here shall close,
An everlasting conscious inanition!
We yearn for speedy death in full fruition,
Dateless oblivion and divine repose.

The images for "Death in Life" continue: where, ordinarily, people affect one another socially in different ways, for good as well as ill, there each only infects the air the others breathe; where people usually attribute majesty and feeling to the heavens, in fact the stars are dead, the heavens "a void abyss"; the city does have a river – but it is The River of the Suicides: even if one does not seek death in it because of "dear foolish friends", at least one can be sure in time of:

That one best sleep which never wakes again.

The first section on the other hand of the narrator's account of his past visit to the city, in which he watches a man endlessly circling round shrines to dead Faith, dead Love, and dead Hope, establishes the basis of the city as being a reversal of Saint Paul's First Epistle to the Corinthians: "And now abideth faith, hope, charity, these three." The man engaged in circling round these shrines offers a metaphor for the meaninglessness of his journey:

Take a watch, erase
The signs and figures of the circling hours,
Detach the hands, remove the dial-face;
The works proceed until run down; although
Bereft of purpose, void of use, still go.

A reference to Paley might seem obvious, but there's also an echo here of Waller's "On the Fear of God". This was one of the poems in the book set for "repetition" lessons to be given in the army schools whilst Thomson was an army schoolmaster:

As clocks, remaining in the skilful hand
Of some great master, at the figure stand,
But, when abroad, neglected they do go,
At random strike, and the false hour do show;
So, from our Maker wandering, we stray,
Like birds that know not to their nests the way.
In Him we dwelt before our exile here,
And may, returning, find contentment there:
True joy may find, perfection of delight,
Behold His face, and shun eternal night.

In fact a process in the poem, of as it were bitterly replying to specific books and passages of literature, runs through "The City of Dreadful Night" from start to finish. And if the basis of the poem is a reply to the Bible, the source of the setting is most obviously Dante. But even though the inscription on the gate of Dante's Hell is used as a prefatory quote to Thomson's poem, the latter embodies within itself negative reversals of positive aspects of Dante's trilogy. Section six of "The City of Dreadful Night" for instance describes how the people in the city cannot even get into Hell – they have no hope left to abandon. And section four contains a reversal of the fortunes of the narrator in Canto Thirty-One of Purgatory, where Matilda drew Dante across the waters of Lethe towards Beatrice: Thomson's narrator is left on the shore, and his final:

But I, what do I here?

Is a bitter echo of Matilda's "Surgi, hef ai?" when she wakened Dante in Canto Thirty-two. Lastly, instead of the great vision of the Queen of Heaven in Canto Thirty-two of Dante's Paradise, there is – Dürer's Melencolia. The references can be multiple: where the action of section four seems to have its source in Dante, the woman herself there seems reminiscent of the Lady in the "Mask of Cupid" set in Busirane's enchanted palace in Book Three of The Faerie Queene. Spenser's "dolefull Lady, like a dreary Spright, / Cald by strone charmes out of eternall night" has, like Thomson's figure bearing "her own burning heart", a wounded breast, where:

> At that wide orifice her trembling hart
> Was drawn forth, and in silver basin layd.

And Spenser's enchanted palace, with its tapestries and altar to Cupid, seems both the source and reverse image of what becomes in Thomson (section ten) a mansion of dead Love, wherein a young man, turning to stone, keeps a vigil by the corpse of the woman he loved. But it mustn't be thought that Thomson, in these "replies" to works of literature, was playing a literary game of spot-the-author. He wasn't writing for examination students, nor attempting to conceal his emotions behind a smokescreen of literary references. For as anyone who reads Thomson's critical essays will discover, Spenser and Dante – like Shakespeare, Burns, Whitman, Heine, Leopardi, De Quincey, Shelley – were people whose works Thomson cared about, passionately. He was always trying to persuade the reader of his essays to read them, and he always wrote with the basic given, that at heart any work of art is one person speaking to another. So his references to previous writers are not indications of his distancing himself, but are indications instead of the true intimacy of his address. He is as it were pulling out of himself those works of literature he loves, and stripping them of their innate optimism before the reader's eyes. But it is not "The Literary Tradition" that he is lacerating in so doing – he is lacerating, in his despair, himself.

But of course not all the authors Thomson cared about showed innate optimism. The pessimistic congruence of thought between Thomson and Leopardi can be seen in Thomson's translations of the Italian; section eleven of "The City of Dreadful Night" with its paradox about the men who are "most rational and yet insane" is reminiscent of a passage of Leopardi which Thomson translated for the National Reformer in 1869:

> For this is the miserable condition of man, and the barbarous teaching of reason, that, our pleasures and pains being mere illusions, the affliction which derives from the certitude of the nullity of all things is evermore and solely just and real. And although if we regulated our life in accordance with the conviction (entiment) of this nullity, the world would come to an end, and we should justly be called mad, it is yet formally certain that this would be a madness reasonable in all regards, and that compared with it all wisdom (tutte le saviezze) would indeed be madness, since everything is done in our world through the simple and continuing ignoring of this universal truth, that all is nothing.

Where section nine, also, extends the metaphor of a purposeless mechanism (as the watch of section two, already quoted) from the individual to the universal:

> "The world rolls round for ever like a mill;
> It grinds out death and life and good and ill;
> It has no purpose, heart or mind or will.
>
> Nay, does it treat him harshly as he saith?
> It grinds him some slow years of bitter breath,
> Then grinds him back into eternal death."

This seems an echo of Carlyle, whose work has many echoes in Thomson's, here being from the Everlasting No of Sartor Resartus:

> To me the Universe was all void of Life, of Purpose, of Volition, even of Hostility: it was one huge, dead, immeasurable Steam-engine, rolling on, in its dead indifference, to grind me limb from limb. O, the vast, gloomy, solitary Golgotha, and Mill of Death!

Yet it's the prevailing refrain of dead Hope, dead Love, dead Faith which holds "The City of Dreadful Night" together. After witnessing (section two) a circling figure visiting the shrines of these, the narrator (and reader) in fact then does likewise. The River of Suicides of sections six and eight can be seen as the shrine of dead Hope; the mansion of section ten, that of dead Love; and the cathedral of sections twelve, fourteen and sixteen, that of dead Faith. But the underlying references in the scene at the cathedral of dead Faith can hardly have been more immediate to Thomson, or to the poem's first readers. "The City of Dreadful Night" first appeared in 1874 in the official organ of the National Secular Society, the National Reformer, edited by Charles Bradlaugh. Yet in section twelve, the congregation's ritualistic rejection of all political activity (besides art, drugs and religion) can be seen as a rejection of the National Secular Society's First Principle: "That the promotion of Human Improvement and Happiness is the highest duty." And the atheist's sermon (section fourteen) which exhorts the congregation not to despair, as they have nothing to fear beyond the grave since "There is no God" – this would certainly have been seen as an allusion to any one of the hundreds of addresses made at the time by Charles Bradlaugh in towns throughout the country. So the congregation's reply (section sixteen) that oblivion beyond the grave does not compensate for unhappiness here and now, would certainly have been seen as a criticism of Bradlaugh's opinions, and those of the mass of secularists. No wonder there were complaints: the man didn't even have faith in the National Secular Society. But with the completion, in section sixteen, of the narrator's visits to the shrines of dead Hope, dead Love, dead Faith, "The City of Dreadful Night", with its interweaving sections of present and past tense, then introduces, in the extraordinary section eighteen, the image of a crawling figure trying to reunite his past with his present – not to go forward, but so that he can return to child- hood, and the womb. The source of this would seem to be Alexander Smith, whose poetry Thomson liked enough to dedicate his "A Happy Poet" to him in 1858. In Smith's "A Life Drama" one finds these words:

> My life was a long dream; when I awoke,
> Duty stood like an angel in my path,
> And seemed so terrible, I could have turned
> Into my yesterdays, and wandered back
> To distant childhood, and gone out to God
> By the gate of birth, not death.

And indeed, in the next section that continues the narrator's account of his visit to the city – the penultimate section in the poem – there is an angel standing before him. And the process by which this angel loses his wings, then his sword, then ends with his head between the sphinx's paws – this represents the process of spiritual, then physical, then mental despair, that parallels the death of faith, hope and love. And this is the initiation rite of the narrator himself.

But to readers familiar with Thomson's complete output, this angel with his sword, facing the sphinx, recalls a similar figure in a previous work by Thomson. In the prose fantasy Sarpolus of Mardon of 1858, published posthumously in Progress magazine in 1887, one finds:

> For the moon was high in heaven, and the stars were count-
> less; – large, beautiful, golden, scintillant, eyes of triumph,
> strange to sorrow, all gazing down from their serene heav-
> en into the Valley of the Shadow of Death. On either side
> of this rock rose two vast images, King and Queen; before
> it was crouched a Mammoth-Sphinx upon whose counte-

nance gazed stedfastly a mightier angel, leaning upon his naked sword, his wings folded in marble patience...

In this fantasy, the family of a dead queen carry her body to be installed on her throne among the dead kings and queens in the Valley of the Shadow of Death. They chant a requiem:

> We must toil with pain and care,
> We must front tremendous Fate,
> We must fight with dark Despair:
> Thou dost dwell in solemn state,
> Couched triumphant, calm and brave,
> In the ever-holy grave.

The names of the three sons who carry her body are Roncel, Armon – and Vanolis. And in the next, and last, section of "The City of Dreadful Night", "Bysshe Vanolis" has placed on her throne above the city the figure of Melencolia. This sad, thinking, introspective figure, who works on in her sorrow, has these qualities in common with one other woman in a poem by Thomson – the woman in the unpublished and untitled poem written, like Sarplus of Mardon, in 1858, and beginning, "The dice to play this dubious game of life". This final reference requires explication. The unfinished poem is in two cantos. In the first, the narrator relates how he was orphaned in early childhood, and taken into the family of a close friend of his late father; this man, a seaman, would often sit by the fire telling the children of the house tales of the sea. The second, unfinished canto describes:

> The Mother – she was very good and sweet
> But always sad

The reason for her sadness being that her father and brother had both been drowned in one ship "Upon the Goodwins". The children didn't understand her suffering, wanting to say:

"You sadden us who want whole worlds of fun!"

Yet when she had received the news of the deaths, she had made no great show of emotion, but walked as if asleep:

With such a fixed & vacant stony gaze
Doing her household work the while she went.

But she was inwardly "frantic" with grief, as:

She and this brother loved each other so

Until at length she filled the "vacuum" in her soul with "mystic love of God", and she learned to welcome misery and "life's thorn-iest paths":

If she might only in pure trance rise
To see her Lord – the Love ineffable
Revealed in glory to her ravished eyes.

If one compares this with the autobiographical letter which Thomson wrote a few months before he died in 1882, one sees that Thomson, the orphan son of a seaman, describes how his mother had "a cloud of melancholy overhanging her; first, perhaps, from the death of her favourite brother, John Parker Kennedy, upon the Goodwin Sands"; again, Thomson notes how she was "mystical-ly inclined with Edward Irving", even "following Irving from the Kirk when he was driven out"; that there was a portrait of Irving at home, and that he used to read "for the imagery" some books of Irving "on the interpretation of prophecy". It was principally the women who first among the Irvingites went into spiritual states of ecstasy, with or without possession of "the gift of tongues". But more pertinent to the analysis here is that the Irvingites largely based their claims that Christ had bequeathed the spiritual gifts of healing, speaking in the tongues, and the power of prophesy, on their interpretation of Saint Paul's First Epistle to the Corinthians. And the power of prophesy required the interpretation of the prophetic books of the Bible, notably, of course, the Book of Revelations. And there, in the Book of Revelations, is the city of God, where "there shall be no night", and "no temple therein" (as God himself will be there); there will be "a pure river of water of life":

> And God shall wipe away all the tears from their eyes; and there shall be no more death, neither sorrow, nor crying, neither shall there be any more pain.

And yet, despite the bitterness of the reply to this, Melencolia works on. With her wings "too impotent", her instruments which only bring bafflement and weariness, and with her expression showing that she understands "all is vanity and nothingness", she embodies the same spiritual, physical and mental despair embodied in the angel of the previous stanza. But still she works on. For what Thomson finally presents is an image of a practical, Calvinistic Madonna. Her name is not Melencolia; her true name is Our Lady of Work-on-Regardless, and it is to she that her subjects look up.

Beckett and Graham
Notes for Edinburgh Review

Some years ago consequent upon illness and accident, the phys-
iological apparatus of the writer of this article was at its nadir in
terms of functional capability. It was reduced, speak we of volition,
to a head on a bed with a pair of arms and hands that moved.
Though the head was incapable of speech, its seeing and hearing
organs performed efficiently. This enabled the head to read, and to
listen to the radio through headphones.

****

In some writers, it's part of the experience of their work to feel that
they are somehow present to the reader. It's to do with the sense
of experiencing the writer's voice, and the terms, literally, of that
voice's address. The writer of course never is physically present to
the reader, but there's a sense somehow that he is what might be
called ego-present. The work has become a model, a little working
model of an ego to which the reader can relate. It can be part of
this model's structure that it seems itself aware that a model is all
that it is.

****

The writer who cleared the way for his voice to come through, it
seems to me, is Beckett. By Beckett I mean the Beckett of the nov-
els, especially the trilogy. At any rate there's a correspondence of
ideas there that's very striking. There's the same games played to
an extent, the same games of voice and landscape.

****

156

Graham casts the writer as dual hero in a double allegory. The hero leaving the real world to journey through metaphor. The allegorical hero journeying through metaphor to arrive at the real world, where the reader or listener is. When Graham operates these two states simultaneously, he creates a state of ambivalence, viscosity of the ego as it were. A fluid state that can inter- mingle a mythic landscape with one from the actual world and its actual people whom he personally knows.

Consciousness of the unattainable particularity of the reader introduces the mock heroic, the mock allegoric. The perpetual invitation to join the game, to merge into this landscape that's half-mythic half real. If you play the game you will in a sense have the ear of the "real" W.S. Graham. This is Malcolm Mooney's Land.

****

Through these headphones one evening came the voice of W.S. Graham, in a programme given over solely to the man reading from his own work. It seemed, to the head on the bed, that the voice coming through the headphones was a voice talking about being a voice: a voice that lived in another man's head, and that was aware in some very gentle but precise way of what a daft concept that was, the concept of a voice living in a head. Part of the daftness was the idea of it living in the speaker's head, and part of it the idea of it living in the listener's – as, at that moment, it was living in the listener's with the headphones.

****

Beckett's prose: some features of style, esp. of later pieces:
long sentences, comma used as rhythmic pause commas used to separate what would normally be separated by a period, colon or semi-colon: these by writers other than Beckett ordinarily used to allow the pause necessary for the tonal shift of a shift in register. The use of the comma has a reductive effect, by giving the same

tone to contradictory arguments. This draws the reader into the writer's collusion with himself about the absurdity of the contradictions that are in a sense flattened by the singleness of tone.

****

Mooney. Probable source Mooney's Bar, Dublin. Malcolm Mooney's Land though is just the name given to the model, the landscape of the ambivalent ego.
The adventure playground, the product of the collusion.

      Reader, it does
Not matter. he is only going to be

Myself and for you slightly you
Wanting to be another.

****

When the writer of this article was once again fully interlocking, vertical and ambulant unsupported, the mouth that now spoke again asked questions of friends and fellow Scottish literati: why, when so many Scottish writers gave so many readings in Scotland, and when so many names were given low or high marks out of ten in so many Whither-Scottish-Literature debates – why, amongst all this blether and activity, W.S. Graham so unnoticed in Scotland? It could not be simply because he was living in Cornwall. That was hardly the other side of the moon.

****

A Diversion Upon Ezra Pound

The foundation voice, patrician

the deliberate cultivation of the oblique: not so as to be obtuse, but because the functional basis of his art is not didactic, but musical the chinese ideogram as the equivalent of a silent bar in music: the eye rests on the ideogram, and the brain is informed, not of what the ideogram "means", but that it is simply some- thing-that-means-something-relevant, that is ancient, that is "graceful". Its function is rhythmic

Pound's art – all this in the Cantos – musical in that its vitality lies on a constant play of differing registers including phoneticised American and the Latin, Greek, French etc., set within the overall patrician. The relation of the verse to the ideograms is in parallel with the relation between high and low register, or better, informal conversational with high culture refs and foreign-language swathes

****

When Graham's Collected Poems appeared in 1979, I was asked to write a review essay, and began work on what I intended to be a lengthy and intricate analysis. But there was a writing block. It seemed to me that to get really into Graham's voice, one would have to get in via the voice of Beckett in the prose works. And to discuss that properly, one would have to get Tristram Shandy off the shelf. And all this seemed to be leading further and further away from actually replying to the voice itself – which I think is what I wanted to do, somehow. I did not want, through a critical essay, to as it were let the voice finish saying its piece, for me to begin a dialogue with someone else about its critical content. That would be for me to shift the grounds of my experience of the voice, to reject it even, in favour of a dialogue with another voice, a third party to the affair.

****

The adventure playground:

paper as snowscape
words as stepping-stones
words as ice bergs.
gaps as holes, pitfalls

Reader under the ice. writer travelling overhead.

****

It was ridiculous. What could this mean? I wanted to write about this man's poetry very much. And yet it seems that deep down, I didn't want to write about it at all. It reached a stasis of some desperation. Sonya (my wife) suggested I go away for four days, to see if I could resolve the matter. And so I found myself in a hotel in Girvan, feeling like someone out of a short story, and hoping that no-one at breakfast or dinner would ask me what I was doing there. I walked a lot by the sea, read and thought a lot about W.S. Graham's poetry.

****

Landscape: seascape, skyscape.
The metaphoric evolution of landscape in his work, in the evolution of the books.
Development from himself seen as landscape, to sea/horizon seen from land (?) to himself on the sea, as fisherman, to the snow, the ice of the page.

In The Nightfishing he presents himself as allegorical hero. In Malcolm Mooney's Land he presents himself as mock allegorical hero. In Implements in their Places he presents the reader as mock allegorical hero.

****

On the Saturday night, the last night of my stay, I went into the hotel bar, from which I'd previously stayed away. Celtic were playing on the television, so I stood at the bar watching the game. This was noticed. But the people who noticed were not bigoted – they told me so themselves. In fact they were so open-minded and friendly, they insisted on introducing me to an old man drinking near the door, who sat there every night, and whom everyone knew was a Roman Catholic. We would get on fine, they said, and left us to it. They're not bigoted here, said the old man whom everyone knew was a Roman Catholic. And so next day I bade farewell to the Royal Hotel, Girvan. My Graham book was covered with marginalia – but the article was unwritten.

****

Some aspects of Beckett's prose style, as in *He is Barehead*.

Beckett's characteristics:	Graham's position after this in italics:
present tense	*yes*
anonymous	*no*
alone	*not necessarily. In fact, never in the sense of his awareness of the reader always. Also poems such as "To Nessie Dunsmuir". But alone in the room as his place of writing, his isolation in existence at the point of creation etc. Also the romantic-turning-to-mock-alle goric isolation of his creating self.*
male	*yes in that Graham is always assumed to be the narrative ego*

clothes in disrepair	*no*
mock philosophising	*no*
landscape, described geometric terms as limiter of persona's movement	*At first it may seem Graham shares this* *characteristic with Beckett, but in fact it's the opposite. In Graham the landscape metaphor is presented as a mode of over coming the limits of communication that are assumed as a given in the first place.*
a "he" located in the head	*definitely, but Graham brings the head of the Other into the equation that is to say the collusion that is Malcolm Mooney's Land*
elaborate mock incompetence	*no, see notes on landscape*

****

Allegorical persona in Beckett can be taken as allegory

—of Man the Male	*Graham No: too particular*
—of Mankind	*No: ditto*
—of the Writer to the Reader	*Yes*

—of the Brain to the Writer, Writing   *Yes*

—of the created fiction, to its creator   *A bit*

—overlap of possibilities of allegory
identifies writer and reader:
an allegory of their being
in the same situation.   *Yes, definitely*

****

I still hadn't written the article when W.S. Graham came at last to read at the Third Eye Centre, on a short reading tour organised by Cencrastus. I was reminded afterwards of a conversation I'd once had with someone who told me that what he wanted to happen, in readings or in theatre, was a moment of a particular quality of silence. I'd known what was meant by that. Graham, in my opinion, hit on this quality of silence at the beginning of his reading in Glasgow, and held it for the best part of an hour. It was something to do with the sense of sharing a heightened state of attentiveness, through language. Apparently the readings at Dundee and Edinburgh were not so successful.

****

Vera Brittain and the Memorial

The service programme at the unveiling of the memorial to Bomber Command on Thursday listed three "philanthropic entrepreneurs" as the principal funders of the 61/2 million pound project. These were billionaires John Caudwell "Lord" Michael Ashcroft, and Richard Desmond.

Caudwell made his fortune as Mr Phones4U, and in 2005 was fined millions of pounds by HMRC for illegally avoiding tax using the Employee Benefit Trust scam for which now-liquidated Glasgow Rangers are under investigation. "Lord" Michael Ashcroft was drafted into the House of Lords in 2000 by William Hague, though he payed no income tax in Britain as he was not a domiciled resident in the UK. His main philanthropic activity in Britain seems to have been pouring money from his untaxed wealth in Belize into Conservative Party funds in marginal constituencies at election time, for which when criticised he said simply that it was not illegal. The third "philanthropic entrepreneur", Richard Desmond, owner of Express Newspapers OK magazine and Channel 5, in 2004 tried to buy the British Daily Telegraph. When told at a meeting with Telegraph executives that the paper was on offer to the German publisher Axelrod, his outburst against Germans as a people and the Telegraph for dealing with them led one executive to state "It was the most grotesque outburst of a mix of slander and racism that I have ever been subjected to. If it had been in a public place he would have been arrested."

The ceremony at the unveiling of the memorial by the Queen was broadcast on BBC television live at noon, then followed at 5pm with an hour-long repeat under the title "Tribute to Bomber Command"; then repeated again at 11pm, then broad- cast yet again the following day on BBC Hard Drive channel at 11pm. But Bomber Command was not always the subject of tribute, even during the war. On November 28th 1943 George Bernard Shaw wrote to the Daily Express "The blitzing of the cities has carried this war to such a climax of infernal atrocity that all recrimination on that score are ridiculous. The Germans will have as big a bill of atrocities against us as we against them if we take them into an impartial court." In Seed of Chaos: What Mass Bombing Really Means, published a year before the bombing of Dresden, Vera Brittain wrote: "The number killed by German air raids on Britain from the beginning of the War up to October 31st, 1943, is just over 50,000. Apart from all that we have done to Italy and to German-occupied countries, our reprisals mean that on Germany alone, up to the end of October 1943, we had already inflicted more than 24 times the suffering that we had endured." The bombing of Hamburg, one of the worst affected, was described in August 1943 as "probably the most complete blotting-out of a city that ever happened" and Reynolds News quoted one report: "We passed whole streets, squares and even districts that had been razed. Everywhere were charred corpses, and injured people had been left unattended. We will remember those Hamburg streets as long as we live...That night the largest workers' district of the city was wiped out."

Of course there were bombing raids on such as Messerschmitt and industrial production factories by Bomber Command. But it was the deliberate whole area "saturation bombing" of towns and cities throughout Germany adopted by Bomber Command's chief of staff Arthur Harris that brought condemnation, and still does. Vera Brittain's words from 1943 still have resonance: "As a Londoner who has been through about 600 raid periods and has spent 18 months as a volunteer fireguard, I have seen and heard enough to know that I at least must vehemently protest when this obscenity of terror and mutilation is inflicted upon the helpless civilians of another country. Nor do I believe that the majority of our airmen who are persuaded that mass bombing reduces the period of their peril really want to preserve their own lives by sacrificing German women and babies, any more than our soldiers would go into action using "enemy" mothers and children as a screen. "What she called the 'horrible facts' about Bomber Command bombing she listed town by town, but these were "not included from sensational motives. They are given in order that you who read may realise exactly what the citizens of one Christian country are doing to the men, women and children of another. Only when you know these facts are you in a position to say whether or not you approve."

Would Vera Brittain—mother of Shirley Williams who in later years became a UK government minister—have approved the memorial unveiled on Thursday? Most definitely not. She would have had sympathy for the friends and relatives of airmen who lost their lives. But the erection of a Bomber Command memorial smells of the attempt to bring "closure", with monarchical seal, to a stubborn never-quite-going-away sense of shame: closure by erasing the perceived relevance, or even awareness, of those "horrible facts" that Vera Brittain and others protested about at the time. It is a monument to monarchism and militarism at a time of economic crisis, a monument for "a sense of national unity" in terms for which those old men in their wheel- chairs are just pawns.

Keeping the Red Flag Flying
The William Gallacher Memorial Library

The William Gallacher Memorial library is in a small, low-ceilinged basement room at the very back of STUC headquarters in Woodside Terrace. A table occupies most of the available floor space. Round the walls are books crammed on shelves put up herself by the voluntary part-time librarian, Audrey Canning. These are some of the books and pamphlets I noted more or less at random on a recent visit.

Mayakovsky's *Lenin*; Magill, Tressell; Biographies of James Connolly; David Kirkwood, *My Life of Revolt*; Tom Bell, *John Maclean, Fighter for Freedom. Speeches from the Dock*, or *Protests of Irish Patriotism* Dublin 1945; shelves of works by and about, Marx, Engels, Lenin. *Britain Without Capitalists* "A Study of what industry in a Soviet Britain could achieve."

Education: *Lies and Hate in Education* by Mark Starr, "Published by Leonard and Virginia Woolf at the Hogarth Press, 1929" – "We have yet to find a textbook which deals fairly with the Indian Mutiny (1857), called by the Indians, incidentally, the War of Independence". *First Principles of Working Class Education* by James Clunie, "Printed and Published by the Socialist Labour Press, 50 Renfrew Street, Glasgow, 1920". Foreword by John Maclean.

Trade Union History: History of the Boilermakers' Society (2 vols); The National Union of Journalists, A Jubilee History 1907-1957; The Rights of Engineers 1944; The History of Cooperation (George Jacob Holyoake); The Blacksmiths' History; Robert Owen and the Owenites in Britain; History of Trade Unionism 1666 – 1920 by Sidney and Beatrice Webb; History of the Kinning Park Cooperative Society, P.J. Dolan; A History of the Scottish Miners.

Among the Miners, Prose and Verse by Thomas Stewart, Larkhall 1893. Includes account of meeting "Davie", i.e. the Cowglen poet David Wingate (see *Radical Renfrew* pp 241-260) as a fireman in a mine in Hamilton: "I can fancy I see him in the grey of a Spring morning, for a fireman has to rise early and go round the workings with a safety lamp before he dares let a man enter".

Russia, a long row:- *The Bolshevik Revolution* (3 vols); *Europe's Debt to Russia; History of the Civil War in the USSR*; The Soviet Union 1935: "a vivid and comprehensive picture of the policy and achievements of the Soviet Union in recent years, bringing the picture down to 1935, the third year of the second five year plan, the chief political task of which is to liquidate capitalist elements and classes in general"; *Soviet Communism, A New Civilisation* (Webb); *An Englishwoman in the USSR* (Violet Lansbury); *Russia without Illusions* 1938; *The USSR Speaks for Itself* 1943; *The Conspiracy Against Russia* 1946; *The Story of the Cossacks; A Time for Peace* (Gorbachev).

Paris under the Commune; From Trotsky to Tito; A History of Hungary; The Tragedy of Chile; How Britain Rules Africa; Vietnam: The Truth; When Japan Goes to War 1935, Mao Tse Tung Selected Works; The Long March – a play by Chen Chi-Tung Peking 1956; Confucius and Modern China.

The Foundations of Imperialist Policy; The Soldiers' Strikes of 1919; Britain, Fascism and the Popular Front; The Bloody Traffic, by Fenner Brockway, 1933: "War and armaments have their roots in the economic system; and it is only by a fundamental change in the economic system that the Bloody Traffic will be ended."

I paid Hitler by "a man who for more than fifteen years backed Hitler and financed his movement", 1941; *The Brown Book of the Hitler Terror and the Burning of the Reichstag,* prepared by an inter- national committee under the presidency of Albert Einstein: "It is always always difficult to obtain authentic information as to what is happening under a well organised terror. Special credit is due to a few of the foreign correspondents in Germany who, at the risk of losing their posts, have contrived to get so much of the truth across the frontier."

A Plea for a State Medical Service by James Erskine MA MB Glasgow 1897; In Place of Fear (signed) by Aneurin Bevan, 1952: "A free health service is pure socialism and as such it is opposed to the pure hedonism of capitalist society."

The Annals of Toil, being Labour History Outlines, Roman and British, in four books; *The Martyrdom of Man; The Freedom of Necessity; The Ruins of Empires* (Volney) – pencilled inside, "from the bookshelf of Uncle Bill" (William Gallacher) first Communist MP in Great Britain died 12ᵗʰ August 1965. *The Purgatory of Suicides,* A Prison Rhyme in Ten Books by Thomas Cooper, Chartist, 1845. "...the fruits of two years and eleven weeks confinement in Stafford Jail"

> What say ye,—that the priests proclaim content?
> So taught their Master,—who the hungry fed
> As well as taught—who wept with men,—and bent,
> In gentleness and love, o'er bier and bed
> Where wretchedness was found, until it fled?
> Rebuked he not the false ones, till his zeal
> Drew down their hellish rage upon his head?—
> And who, that yearns for world-spread human weal
> Doth not, ere long, the weight of priestly vengeance feel?

Leaves from a Prison Diary, or Lectures to a "solitary" audience, by Michael Davitt, Founder of the Land League, 1885: "To the memory of the little confiding friend whose playful moods and loving familiarity helped to cheer the solitude of a convict cell; to my pet blackbird "Joe", these prison jottings are dedicated.... He would stand upon my breast as I lay in bed in the morning, and awaken me from sleep...... One evening, as "Joe" sat upon his perch, it occurred to me to constitute him chairman and audience of a course of lectures; and with him constantly before me as a representative of my fellow creatures, I jotted down what I have substantively reproduced in the following pages."

A row of Thinkers Library; of bound *Labour Monthly*; of *Modern Quarterly*; of Left Book Club editions: *Poems of Freedom* 1938, introduction by W.H. Auden; *The Road to Wigan Pier* (Orwell) 1937.

Foursom Reel: A Collection of New Poetry by John Kincaid, George Todd, F.J. – (Freddy)- Anderson, Thurso Berwick, 1949. Preface by MacDiarmid. *Poems of a Glasgow Worker,* by Freddy Anderson 1952. Preface: "The poems in this little book spring from the struggles of the people to make Britain a land of real democracy...

Rationalist Press Association magazines; a run of Left Review from the Thirties. The minutes, programmes, and some manuscripts submitted for consideration, to the Edinburgh Labour Festival Committee in connection with the Edinburgh People's Festival of the early fifties – a forerunner to today's Fringe. The committee included Norman Buchan, Hugh MacDiarmid and Hamish Henderson.

The Revolution, June 1918: "A Capitalist judge and a jury of petty businessmen have sentenced John Maclean to penal servitude for five years."

The Red Dawn, monthly, twopence. March 1919: "The Proletarian College was instituted on Sunday 12th January 1919 by our comrade Tom Anderson, principal and founder, at our headquarters 17 Oswald Street, Glasgow; our Sunday class is unique, fully 130 being present at the first meeting. Our text- book is *The State, its Origin and Function,* by William Paul, and our teacher is Johnny Maclean of Bridgeton. Before he is done with the State, we will have some able young men and women in the city of Glasgow.... Evening classes at headquarters are being well attended. The teachers for elementary economics are comrades James Connal and James Anderson. Class meets every Monday at 8 p.m. *A Worker Looks at History,* by Mark Starr, has been taken up by our principal and the class is every Thursday at 8 p.m." Slogans at the foot of each page of *The Red Dawn :*—When your master calls you, you must go— Consider the lilies of the field – then look at the Working Class— The term capital has no equivalent in the Greek and Latin tongues— The prime minister was exhausted, and he sat down— When they pray they don't mean anything— The conscript is a wage slave in uniform— The ethics of religion are:- Donations thankfully received— "Work for the night is coming" was written before the night-shift was invented— The police are your master's watchdogs— When the anthem plays, laugh— When the Gaffer sleeps in, it seems like a holiday— Law is the Army and the Navy— Look up, there he's coming— When you see a man with medals, pity him—

Socialist Poems Suitable for Recitations, Glasgow Labour Literature Society, 1893; The Proletarian Catechism by Tom Anderson, one penny, 1933: The International Song Book; The Rebels' Ceilidh Song Book; Songs for Pioneers; Songs of the People; Songs of the Internationale; Socialist Sunday School Song Books, 1925.

This library, founded on a personal collection, is within the great tradition of freethinking, working-class libraries that have kept intellectual debate and democratic discussion alive outside the usual institutions. The South Wales Miners' Library, the Library of the Bishopsgate Institution, the Working Class Movement Library at Salford, are others. Donations of books or requests by researchers regarding consultation or information from the library at STUC headquarters, should be first addressed in writing to the librarian.

Six Glasgow Poems

About a year after I had written my *Six Glasgow Poems* in the winter of 1968/69, I went to give a reading including these poems to a group of teachers and students in a teacher training college. I arrived late to find the teachers discussing "whether a person should be allowed to write like that." I was given to understand that my writing was not just "bad English", but "bad Scots"— which was even worse. That kind of attitude I was to encounter quite a few times in coming years, and it was to politicise me—or make my politics that were already implicitly in my poems increasingly more articulate to myself and in my subsequent work. After *Six Glasgow Poems* I had to find out why some people seemed to hate what I had written and to feel the need to sneer at it so much. I had to work my way through to a clarity about the whole business of hierarchies of British diction, of historic but still sometimes beneath-the-surface racism and snobbishness in Scotland towards nineteenth century immigrant Irish and other working-class incomers who had "spoiled" a "pure" Scots language which had never even existed as "pure" in the first place. Languages don't—at least outside of books.

"The Good Thief" was the first of the poems to arrive when I was writing the sequence. I don't remember the "inspiration" particularly, only that I had got very fed up with the presentation of Glasgow speakers as somehow cuddly, bowdlerised, always the amusing "Other" wheeled on by an of-course not working-class author to be shared with an of-course not working-class reader. Looking back, it reminds me of my feelings then about the Glasgow psychiatrist R D Laing's great book *The Divided Self* which came out in the early sixties, in which he discussed the 176 triangle of complicity between doctor and family, pathologising the speech of the "patient" schizophrenic as behaviour-pattern merely demonstrating Otherness, an intrinsic lack of subjective ontological validity.

I loved Laing's book, which I kept giving away to others. I don't think it influenced my ideas on the literary representation of urban speech, but looking back I see a definite congruence arrived at my thinking.

I had to make the fact of the sound of the diction exact, since that was exactly what was always left out. That indeed was wherein the politics of the whole business lay. Ironically, since these were the very sounds that had come down over centuries perhaps from as far as Dunbar's time, but were now derided on grounds of vocabulary, or "lack" of it, or use of glottalisation, by people who in comparative terms more often as not had hardly a Scottish sound in their mouths—though banging on about "Scots" might be one of their favourite drums.

I have mentioned hostility the Glasgow poems aroused, but there was much positive response also. When the booklet was newly out, a woman came into the bookshop I worked in and told me that her husband had nearly fallen out of his bed laughing reading the poems, though he was ill with influenza. Then an actor a couple of years later told me that when he put on a staged presentation of "The Good Thief" at a show in Edinburgh, a woman near the front of the audience sat crying throughout the performance. In my more comforting moments, I like to think that both these people who encountered the work so differently nonetheless understood what it was actually about.

Forty Years On
(published in Glasgow University magazine)

Professor Tom Leonard, who retires from his position as Professor of Creative Writing in September, recalls his editorship of GUM forty years ago and gives his views on news reporting.

It's forty years ago in 1969 that I was student editor of Glasgow University Magazine and attempted to publish in its pages a little group of dialect poems I had newly written called Six Glasgow Poems. But the university printer refused to print them, prob- ably because the language used by the characters in the poems included swearwords. So I xeroxed the poems onto sheets using the SRC photocopying machine, and put Six Glasgow Poems as an insert into every single copy of the new GUM that went out. Shortly af- ter their clandestine appearance between the pages of GUM, the poems were published as a booklet which went into reprint after a couple of months, and Six Glasgow Poems have remained in print in one publication or another more or less ever since.

The poems at the outset met with a strong positive response. But it was an equally strong negative response from some self-appoint- ed guardians of the nation's literary culture that actually astonished me. Not only were these poems "bad English" according to these snooty outraged ones, they were "bad Scots" into the bargain— which apparently was even worse. I didn't at all realise the full po- litical nature of what I had become involved in, and the forces that I had now engaged with and would be engaged with over the next four decades, about the hierarchy of different language varieties in Britain in terms of power and status; and the politics of the society that this situation reflected.

Editing GUM had introduced me a little to the world of student politics. At any rate I attended a couple of SRC meetings, though my only memory is of being wholly taken aback by the way peo- ple would stand in a debate and totally slag somebody off, which accused might be sitting a few yards away nonchalantly reading a newspaper or talking to a pal. It seemed an extraordinary way of behaving. Politics as generally understood by the term didn't mean much to me at the time, I was much more interested in the exciting things that had been happening in American poetry in the sixties, developments that influenced me in finding my own voice as a writer. I did as editor kind of political debate going about the of GUM try to get some Middle East, as much to enlighten myself as anybody else. I let it be known I would give equal space to two students if they could put the separate Israeli and Arab points of view regarding the latest instalment of war there and its aftermath, and explain what it was all about. But nobody took me up on the offer.

The end of my editorship of GUM after a year was also the end of my first spell at Glasgow University. I hadn't passed enough exams to be able to continue. I loathed the exam system and had parodied it in a GUM editorial with a collage of quotes implicitly comparing the university exam system in Literature with one whereby as one psychologist had written "mental hospitals actually make people worse, by classifying harmless eccentrics as lunatics and teaching them the appropriate role behaviour". Later I analysed the metaphor "the language of the gutter" and what attitudes that metaphor stood for and perpetuated. The culture and linguistic expression of university exams I thought not only intrinsically and narrowly middle-class in a way as to make someone like myself from a working class background feel alienated; it was a structured defence-formation against the subversive nature of the creative spirit itself: "Being versus Having, that's the battle that's been going on since the year dot; and every time an artist's scored to win the match for Being, the shouts haven't died down but the critics have equalised. But the critics still have to fight it out amongst themselves to decide who scored the equaliser, and the university functions by "training" people in spotting who did."

I was trying just to work things out about my own language and culture and its evident oil and water conflict with the language and culture of official institutions. Language was a political matter, I was forced to confront, and to try to articulate more clearly. I had begun to be aware of "the news" as the most omnipresent language construction in people's everyday lives, effortlessly forming their casual opinion of what was going on in

"the world". I began to listen to different broadcasters. With the outbreak of the Troubles in Ireland, Bloody Sunday found me comparing the language and choice of words used by different reporters in different news bulletins from the BBC, from RTE— Irish Radio—and from AFN, the American forces network. Different broadcasters focused on different primary images: one of a priest trying to save a shot victim, another of crowds supposedly starting the trouble. The different effects created by these choices were clear evidence that the notion of an "objective" news presentation was baloney. A news bulletin was, and is, a language construct. It is not a sort of vacuum in the aether into which Truth rushes and sorts itself out in order of moral and political significance. But that cosy legend has an attractive pull. After all the BBC is the best broadcasting company in the world. Doesn't the BBC itself say so?

I had moved on. I had come to recognise that "managing the language environment" is a crucial and central function of government, and that the idea of genuine separation does not stand up to scrutiny. That trusty old friend, the "objective voice of truth" had a part to play in instilling confidence, as a poem of

1976 I wrote sent up:

    this is thi
    six a clock
    news thi
    man said n
    thi reasona talk wia
    BBC accent
    iz coz yi
    widny wahnt
    mi ti talk
    aboot thi
    trooth wia

voice lik
wanna yoo
scruff. if
a toktaboot
thi trooth
lik wanna yoo
scruff yi
widny thingk
it wuz troo.
 jist wanna yoo
scruff tokn.

That was how the poem began. The full poem has been in the
GCSE syllabus in England and Wales now for about nine years. I
sometimes joke when introducing it at readings, that if I had re-
alised this poem was going to make me the money it has, I would
have written one about the one o'clock news as well. The English
syllabus at least recognises the poem as part of a debate about the
status and power of nonstandard languages in Britain, of region
and/or class; in Scotland it would never have made it onto the
syllabus without disappearing into some sterile tread- mill about
"the Scots language".

"Managing the language environment" reminds me of a trip I
made with my wife and family to the then Soviet Union in 1989,
a year before the Communist system was destined to collapse. We
had a couple of days in Moscow, three days in what was then called
Leningrad, and nine days in Yalta in the Ukraine. The airport used
in the Ukraine was at Simferopol—the place from where, about 84
years earlier, my wife's Jewish forebears, on her mother's side, had
fled the pogroms. We didn't get the chance to explore Simferopol.
But what I do mostly remember about that holiday, apart from a
visit to Chekhov's house, was my attempt in Leningrad to listen
to the hotel radio. From one end of the radio wave band to the
other there was only one station to be heard, which I gathered to
be Radio Moscow. The rest of the band was silent, as creepy and
eloquent a silence as one could ever hear.

How different in our own country. The airwaves awash with "rolling news", the most popular radio stations interrupted every fifteen minutes by "news updates". It is virtually impossible to get away from "the news". Even standing in a bank or post office queue, a plasma screen as likely as not is likely to be bearing down on one with the rolling 24x7 output of Sky News, or BBC 24. And yet—what do I hear?

I hear silence.

Recently at a benefit for the displaced and injured in the bombing of Gaza this January, I told the audience it would be a more ethically appropriate and efficient way of finding out what was happening in the Middle East if one stuck one's head in an aluminium bucket, than it would be if one listened to the BBC news. With one's head in a bucket one would at least be aware that all one could hear was silence—whereas listening to "the" news, or reading our valiant Fourth Estate, the real silence about what was going on would be one of which the reader would be unaware—indeed presentation would be such as to obscure the fact that "silence" was the principle most relevant ingredient.

But things have changed, again. We have the internet, and there is an amount of power to bypass and even ignore the Official Word, and the official absence of word. There are other sources of information. Such access one can be certain that some people in power do not welcome. The criminalisation of such access would only continue that policy of suppression of dissent whose history comfortably extends back into the nineteenth century and beyond. "The Mob" (i.e. the populace) are not to be trusted. More databases!! More DNA!! Always there is the simple decisive courage of ordinary people, who just will not have it. The courage of the creative against the negative, of people putting others before themselves, knowing and believing that all other people are as fully human as they are. It's quite a simple thing, in a way. Such is the example of the Israeli Mordechai Vanunu, who, being totally opposed to nuclear arms and finding that the nuclear plant he was a technician in was making them, exposed this state secret to British journalists. For this he ended up serving eighteen years in jail, much of it in solitary. The students of Glasgow University to their great credit elected him Rector, though he was unable to attend the installation ceremony in 2005, still being refused permission to travel abroad. So there was a ceremony of appointment "in absentia", his rectorial robe draped over an empty chair. I wrote a poem for the occasion and read it from the platform. I dedicated it to Mordechai Vanunu, but it's not just about him, it's about all of us as human, I think.

Being a Human Being
(for Mordechai Vanunu)

not to be complicit
not to accept everyone else is silent it must be alright

not to keep one's mouth shut to hold onto one's job
not to accept public language as cover and decoy

not to put friends and family before the rest of the world
not to say I am wrong when you know the government is wrong

not to be just a bought behaviour pattern
to accept the moment and fact of choice

I am a human being
and I exist

a human being
and a citizen of the world

responsible to that world
—and responsible for that world

CODA

Autumn Leaves

The last thing I always wanted to do was to define something. Literally. Sometimes the process of creativity is the process of defining, it turns out. So creativity is process, that is the point. A commodity driven society will hold that creativity is measured in outcomes. Creativity is on the side of being, not having.

I don't fear ageing in that there is only the present day, take what you have. Like many I have COPD and have found out what "waterboarding" feels like when I had an infection last year. Avoiding infection in cold damp Glasgow is a base line now. My mother's voice in my head is saying We huvvny died o winter yet.

I have never spelled out my motives for writing. I don't even think of it as something that has motives, like murder. But a few of what seem to me the best poems I have written have been written out of the sense there was nothing else to do. Without whatever it was I was in pursuit of, the silence without it could no longer be a given for me. Other poems began in anger and led to enjoyment, sometimes.

Just following the words, though occasionally again commissions.

In the years immediately preceding my 70th birthday I translated Brecht's *Mother Courage and her Children* and worked on my website journal that had daily reactions to and analyses of events political, musical, personal; put up poems, posters, recordings. An open private space, used as exploration towards if anything, a retrospective of a person in their time and place. When I was about sixteen I was given a five year diary by my sister that had a lock on it. I decided I would write each day and not read it until at the end of the process I could find out the sum and constancy of what was there. My web journal another version, fifty years later.

Once daily I usually go out to do a bit of shopping and go to a cafe where I sit and read, or I go there with my wife Sonya, or meet a friend.

The space where the creativity happens on the page if it is to happen on the page, is usually when I get up between about four in the morning and work to maybe six. I have recently gone through my computer making a selection of letters over 25 years and put it on my website. In letters often I would be working out my thoughts. Writing is writing no matter what. In compiling the selection I also had in mind something like the web journal, in the letters' collocation. The record of a particular person who happened to be there in that place, at that time.

Every year I set myself to make a seasonal card for a small circle of friends. This year it was a card with photo of a lamp- post shining at night, and a poem set alongside it. I had made the lamp image by taking a photo on the web page that came up after I had Googled "streetlamp" in Google images, then extracting the lamp area of the photo using Photoshop. The resultant image was thin and vertical. Around the streetlamp showed darkness apart from the light at its base. The image with poem I printed onto blank card using my computer printer, and on the other side of the card I printed seasonal greetings from my wife Sonya and myself.

I also made an e-card version to attach to an email for despatch to a bunch of people, the season's greetings being beneath the image and poem, around which I inserted a border. The email itself read "Poem written a while back when I had walked under a lamp on a path by the Kelvin Walkway and saw the silhouette of my father bunnit and all."

The poem which the image accompanied was as follows:

passing through

it is my father's shade
that lengthens before me
then fades to the dark
where the shade has gone
and to which I walk

AFTERWORD :
'Tom'[1]

---

1   This memoir derives from the address given by James Kelman at the funeral of Tom Leonard, his friend and comrade of forty-five years.

Tom Leonard never represented any group or party in his life. He is the embodiment of the individual: the living, breathing unique self. Spiritually, existentially. People from throughout Scotland, Ireland, England and Wales would have wanted to be here today; from different parts of the world. Many are. His life exemplified the courage and the heroism of one person, one human being. This is expressed in him, in his self and in his work – a body of work that is unsurpassable.

What are the terms we apply, the attributes of Tom Leonard? Integrity, honesty, passion; absolute commitment, absolute faith, faith in life, in the living. Was there ever a more spiritual man?

We had a few strong individuals in and around the city, fifty years ago. We still have. People prepared to enter the struggle, to return the fight, to carry it forward. Tom was one, at the age of twenty-one or twenty-two, he was an instant hero with his Six Glasgow Poems. And for more than fifty years he has remained a hero.

Tom never stopped. Through thick and thin, good health and bad he kept on working, helping, supporting, never afraid to nail his colours to the mast. In solidarity. He fought for what he believed. He met everything head on, everything and everyone. As far as 'flyting' goes Tom led the field, up there with old Dunbar.

Those times one thought, Tom Tom, take it easy, they aren't worth it. But for Tom everyone was worth it. He did take it on. Everyone *deserved* to be taken on. People he knew as enemies. Each one was a human being. And *deserved* to be treated as a human being. So Tom did. And he waded right in, punch for punch. What do ye mean? What do ye mean what do ye mean! Hang on a minute! Ye're no getting away with that!

And in he went, all that physical and emotional energy, intellectual passion, engaging, confronting. Tom gave it all, and we worried for him, we worried for him.

Tom loved many people. And many of those are discovered in his work: composers, musicians, visual artists; doctors and philosophers, theologians, poets, playwrights; prose-writers clunking along ... Plus assorted members of Celtic Football Club.

Okay 1967 was important, the European Cup and all that. But 1957! What about that! Tom's amazing fitba scrapbook that he kept from boyhood! Some of you here today have seen it. Mochan, Peacock, Evans, Fernie, Wilson, Collins, McPhail – Charlie Tully! In 1957 Tom's favourite song was a calypso. I'll gie ye the first line:

Oh Island in the Sun,
(Celtic seven, Rangers one.)

Apologies to Harry Belafonte who wrote and sang the original; thanks for the melody.

Tom's tradition takes from anywhere and gives to anyone. The local is primary. Tom insists on this, both as starting place and as end place. The local is the universal. It's not going anywhere. True universalism. This is a living community, and we fight for the living community; a community of free-thinking individuals. In solidarity.

This is what makes his work so radical, so dangerous; anathema to authority. That is Tom's tradition. This is how I see it. Tom's lifework. All of it. His beautiful poetry; the drawings, posters and sketches, cartoons; songs and music, his wonderful satire, brilliant essays; and the blogs, and the journal. All of it. Leave it alone. It's one thing. That is Tom's work, his lifework. Don't touch it, don't divide it. It is one thing. It is a complete thing of one man. Don't meddle with that.

Aonghas Macneacail, friend of Tom for fifty years, doesn't see Tom as a pioneer at all, he is the pinnacle. I see this too. One cannot reach beyond.

Tom was a master. In recent times he was back working on Places of the Mind, his book on B. V. Thomson and these preoccupations Tom held from boyhood: good and evil, innocence, guilt, right and wrong; sin *a priori*, freedom and providence; where an older philosophy meets existentialism: Augustine; Eriugena, Duns Scotus, Aquinas, Kierkegaard, Buber. More heroes. *Many* masters.

That is the tradition.

Its heart is a community, an ever-expanding community. Nobody is excluded. Self-identify! Whoever ye are! We may not separate literature, art, politics, music, theology, science: teaching as demystification, tradition bearing; generation through generation.

Where truth is authorized, 'it is not necessary to think,' as somebody once said.

People cope with authorized 'truth' from various sources, sources that may be vouchsafed by society but which individuals learn not to trust, to seek clarification. Authorities aren't keen on clarity. They see it as a challenge. Heresy! Let the punishment begin: marginalization, censorship, suppression, withdrawal of resources. People learn to haud their wheesht. Others persist and take it as far as they can, they begin from the beginning: how they speak, how they think, how they breathe.

How is your breath this morning?

Tom's presence ... Did he write that?

No, I did. Tom is that kind of writer. We work away on our own writing and become aware of his presence, his patterns of thought. He was a Christian some of the time, an atheist some of the time, an agnostic some of the time, and for much of the time antagonistic to each of those, reaching to where the negation entitles its own field, a belief-system in itself.

What do ye mean truth? Your truth is not my truth. If I say truth as we know truth it is not the same as you saying truth as we know truth. There is this difference between you and me. And everybody else. And people to come and people who ever have been, there is this difference, between every single person, every single living breathing thing: everything, in one way or another, there is this. What is this? Patterns of thought, echoes of Tom. It is the striving itself, at the level he brings to it, that provides the profundity.

He was a master. And we need to be strong enough to say that of him, to honour him; to honour him for what he was and what he is. I doubt I could have said that to him. I doubt he would have coped with it. In the midst of his own self-belief, the essential self-belief without which his great work would not exist, in the midst of the faith he had in that, he had such humility.

Yes he was a master. But one of many. That is the strength of this tradition. From anywhere and everywhere, and from any historical period: take from it and give within it.

Tom is not only a major literary figure but of such power in the personal sense. His impact on people's lives is massive. For some of us the shock was heightened: we had been in touch with him in recent weeks, recent days even. We knew how poorly he had been but it was his indomitability; spiritual, intellectual. If Tom said he wasn't keeping great then we can make a guess about the reality, the sheer physical assault on the body he endured.

It's difficult for people to come to terms with what has happened. At the same time, he leaves a body of work that ensures his presence; the dialogue continues. One to one. That is Tom. Ye want to talk with Tom? Go to his work. How do you cope with the world? Do what Tom did. Don't hide. Do the best ye can.

If all human beings are unique the story of each person's life is unique. In answer to how many stories are there in the world we say as many as there are human beings; at least as many as there are human beings; more than there are human beings, as many as need be, and on we go.

Pick yerself up and get on with it. That is what Tom Leonard did, that is his lesson, that is Tom's lesson. What more can there be than one human being doing his best, doing her best, forever and ever. That is Tom Leonard.

James Kelman

NOTES

"Opinion of the Press" is a longer version of a poem from "Sour-scenes of Scottish Literary Life", published in *Reports from the Present* (1995).

"The Aquarian" was published in *Eddie's Own Aquarius*, Cahermee publications (2005), celebrating Eddie Linden's 70th birthday and his editorial work for *Aquarius* magazine.

"For Eddie as always, on his 90th (for Eddie Morgan)", was included in *Eddie @ 90* (Scottish Poetry Library and Mariscat Press, 2010, Robyn Marsack and Hamish Whyte, eds).

Being Scottish" and "thinks" came from the "new unpublished" folder on Tom's computer. "The Eff Word" was unpublished written in 2005.

The rest of the poems were published on Tom's web journal [www.tomleonard.co.uk], 2009-14.

"My Way" is from the revue *Tickly Mince*, 1982, co-written with Liz Lochhead and Alasdair Gray. It is meant to be sung to the tune of "My Way" by Frank Sinatra.

"Ezra Pound. Pound and Zukofsky", "The Chatto Book of West Indian-British Poetry.", "The Collected Poems of William Carlos

Williams", "Beckett and Graham", and "Mater Tenebrarum", were for the *Edinburgh Review* in the 1980s.

"Two Monologues and Two Scenes" was published in *Chapman* magazine in 1986.

"Norman MacCaig: Collected Poems", "The Lord Chamberlain's Blue Pencil", "Tony Benn: Diaries 1977 – 80," "Furtwängler", "Kathy Galloway: Love Burning Deep", were all review pieces for the *Glasgow Herald* during the 1980 – 90s.

The "Six Glasgow Poems" essay was written in 2007.

"Forty Years On" was published in Glasgow University magazine (2009).

"Vera Brittain and the Memorial" was a published on Tom's web journal in 2012.

"The Cesspit and the Sweetie Shop" was featured in *The Scotsman* (2014).

"Autumn Leaves" was written for Playspace publications, Larry Butler (2018).

Printed in Great Britain
by Amazon

35217701R00117